Eight Sabbats
for Witches

By the same authors:

WHAT WITCHES DO
THE WITCHES' GODDESS
THE WITCHES' WAY

Eight Sabbats
for Witches

*and rites for Birth, Marriage
and Death*

by

Janet & Stewart Farrar

with line illustrations by
Stewart Farrar and photographs
by Ian David & Stewart Farrar

PHOENIX PUBLISHING INC.

PHOENIX PUBLISHING INC.
Portal Way
P.O. Box 10
Custer, Washington USA 98240

ISBN 0-919345-26-3

Cover design by Rick Testa

Printed in the U.S.A.

To our dear friend
KATH D'EATH, née CARTER
(1905–76)

"And ye shall meet, and know,
and remember,
and love them again."

"I wish there were some way of reconciling formal education and natural knowing. Our inability to do this is a terrible waste of one of our most valuable resources. There is a fund of knowledge, a different kind of information, common to all people everywhere. It is embodied in folklore and superstition, in mythology and old wives' tales. It has been allowed to persist simply because it is seldom taken seriously and has never been seen to be a threat to organized science or religion. It is a threat, because inherent in the natural way of knowing is a sense of rightness that in this time of transition and indecision could serve us very well."

Lyall Watson, *Gifts of Unknown Things*

"If we are to get out of the mess to which civilized ignorance has brought us, we must prepare ourselves, in some ways at least, for the return of paganism."

Tom Graves, *Needles of Stone*

Contents

Acknowledgements

We would like to thank Doreen Valiente for her invaluable help in providing information, for permission to reproduce several ritual passages which she herself wrote for Gardner's Book of Shadows, and for reading our manuscript before publication.

We are grateful to Messrs. Faber & Faber for permission to quote extensively from Robert Graves' *The White Goddess*.

We are also grateful to the Society of the Inner Light for permission to use passages from Dion Fortune's *The Sea Priestess* as part of our Handfasting Ritual.

Introduction

Modern witchcraft, in Europe and America, is a fact. It is no
longer an underground relic of which the scale, and even the
existence, is hotly disputed by anthropologists. It is no longer
the bizarre hobby of a handful of cranks. It is the active religious
practice of a substantial number of people. Just how large a
number is not certain, because Wicca, beyond the individual
coven, is not a hierarchically organized religion. Where formal
organizations do exist, as in the United States, this is for legal
and tax reasons, not for dogmatic uniformity or the numbering
of members. But the numbers are, for example, enough to
support a variety of lively periodicals and to justify the publication of an ever-growing body of literature, on both sides of the
Atlantic; so a reasonable estimate would be that the active
adherents of Wicca now number tens of thousands, at the very

least. And all the evidence suggests that the number is growing steadily.

Wicca is both a religion and a Craft—aspects which Margaret Murray has distinguished as "ritual witchcraft" and "operative witchcraft". As a religion—like any other religion, its purpose is to put the individual and the group in harmony with the Divine creative principle of the Cosmos, and its manifestations, at all levels. As a Craft, its purpose is to achieve practical ends by psychic means, for good, useful and healing purposes. In both aspects, the distinguishing characteristics of Wicca are its Nature-based attitude, its small-group autonomy with no gulf between priesthood and 'congregation', and its philosophy of creative polarity at all levels, from Goddess and God to Priestess and Priest.

This book is concerned with the first aspect—Wicca as a religion, ritually expressed.

Witches, on the whole, enjoy ritual—and they are naturally joyous people. Like worshippers of other religions, they find that appropriate ritual uplifts and enriches them. But their rituals tend to be more varied than other faiths', ranging from the formal to the spontaneous and differing also from coven to coven, according to their individual preferences and the schools of thought (Gardnerian, Alexandrian, 'Traditional', Celtic, Dianic, Saxon and so on) on which they have based themselves.

But as the twentieth-century Wiccan revival matures (and in many covens passes into its second generation), the inter-school acrimony which marred its early years has considerably diminished. Dogmatists still slang each other in the periodicals—but increasingly their dogmatism is condemned by other correspondents as pointlessly disruptive; and most ordinary covens are simply bored by it. The years have taught them that their own path works—and if (like our own coven) they have friends of other paths, they have also come to understand that *those* paths work too.

Out of this greater mutual tolerance has grown an increased awareness of Wicca's common basis, its essential spirit which has little to do with the details of form. Also, with the exchange of ideas both through the printed word and through more open personal contact, there is a growing body of shared tradition on which everyone may draw.

It is as a contribution to this growth that we offer our present book. To be valid, and useful, any such contribution must be a branch arising healthily out of the parent trunk of our racial history, as well as the specific forms of Wiccan practice as it now stands (in our case, the Gardnerian/Alexandrian forms); and this is what we have worked to achieve.

Fortunately, a framework exists which is common to all Wiccan paths, and indeed to many others: the Eight Festivals.

The modern witches' calendar (whatever their 'school') is rooted, like that of their predecessors through untold centuries, in Sabbats, seasonal festivals which mark key points in the natural year, for Wicca, as we have stressed, is a Nature-oriented religion and Craft. And since, for witches, Nature is a many-levelled reality, their 'natural year' includes many aspects—agricultural, pastoral, wildlife, botanical, solar, lunar, planetary, psychic—the tides and cycles of which all affect or reflect each other. The Sabbats are the witches' way of celebrating, and putting themselves in tune with, these tides and cycles. For men and women are also a part of many-levelled Nature; and witches strive, consciously and constantly, to express that unity.

The witches' Sabbats are eight:

IMBOLG, 2nd February (also called Candlemas, Oimelc, Imbolc).

SPRING EQUINOX, 21st March (Alban Eilir).

BEALTAINE, 30th April (Beltane, May Eve, Walpurgis Night, Cyntefyn, Roodmass).

MIDSUMMER, 22nd June (Summer Solstice, Alban Hefin; also sometimes called Beltane).

LUGHNASADH, 31st July (August Eve, Lammas Eve, Lady Day Eve).

AUTUMN EQUINOX, 21st September (Alban Elfed).

SAMHAIN, 31st October (Hallowe'en, All Hallows Eve, Calan Gaeaf).

YULE, 22nd December (Winter Solstice, Alban Arthan).

Of these, Imbolg, Bealtaine, Lughnasadh and Samhain are the 'Greater Sabbats'; the Equinoxes and Solstices are the 'Lesser Sabbats'. (The actual dates of Equinoxes and Solstices may vary by a day or two in traditional usage, and also from year to year in astronomical fact, while the Greater Sabbats tend to involve both the 'Eve' and the following 'Day'.) The solar-astronomical Lesser Sabbats are both older and newer than the natural-fertility Greater Sabbats—older, in that they were the highly sophisticated preoccupation of the mysterious Mega-lithic peoples who pre-dated Celt, Roman and Saxon on Europe's Atlantic fringe by thousands of years; newer, in that the Celts—perhaps the biggest single influence in giving to the Old Religion the actual ritual shape in which it has survived in the West—were not solar-oriented and celebrated only the Greater Sabbats, until what Margaret Murray has called the "solstitial invaders" (the Saxon and other peoples who swept westward with the decay of the Roman Empire) met and interacted with the Celtic tradition. And even they brought only the Solstices: "The Equinoxes," says Murray, "were never observed in Britain." (For some thoughts on how they subse-quently entered British folklore, see page 72—and remember that, since Murray, more has been learned about Megalithic astronomy, which may well have left buried folk-memories to be revived later.)

All this is reflected in the fact that it is the Greater Sabbats which have Gaelic names. Of the various forms which witches use, we have chosen the Irish Gaelic ones, for personal and historical reasons—personal, because we live in Ireland, where those forms have living meanings; historical, because Ireland was the only Celtic country never to be absorbed by the Roman Empire, and so it is in Ireland's mythology and in her ancient language that the lineaments of the Old Religion can often be most clearly discerned.[1] Even the Celtic Church remained stubbornly independent of the Vatican for many centuries.[2]

---

1. Ireland virtually escaped the horrors of the witchcraft persecution. From the fourteenth to the eighteenth century only a handful of trials for witchcraft are recorded. "In England and Scotland during the mediaeval and later periods of its existence, witchcraft was an offence against the laws of God and man; in Celtic Ireland dealings with the unseen were not regarded with such abhorrence, and indeed had the sanction of custom and antiquity" (St John D. Seymour, *Irish Witchcraft and Demonology*, p. 4—and Seymour was a Christian theologian writing in 1913). Nor is there any evidence of torture being used to extract evidence in the few Irish witchcraft trials, except for the flogging in 1324 of Petronilla of Meath, Dame Alice Kyteler's servant, on the orders of the Bishop of Ossory, and that "seems to have been carried out in what may be termed a purely unofficial manner" (*ibid.*, pp. 18–19).

Moreover, Ireland is still predominantly agricultural and a community of human dimensions, where folk-memories still flourish that have elsewhere died in the concrete jungle. Scratch the topsoil of Irish Christianity, and you come at once to the bedrock of paganism. But the use of Irish Gaelic forms is only *our* choice, and we would not wish to impose it on anyone else.

Why have we written this book, with its detailed suggestions for Sabbat rituals, if we do not wish to 'impose' patterns upon other witches—which we most certainly do not?

We have written it because eight years of running our own coven has convinced us that some such attempt is needed. And we think it is needed because the Book of Shadows, Gerald Gardner's anthology of inherited rituals which—with Doreen Valiente's help—he linked together with modern elements to fill in the gaps and make a workable whole, is surprisingly inadequate in one aspect: the Eight Sabbats.

The modern Wiccan revival, so rapidly expanding, owes a tremendous debt to Gerald Gardner, however much he may have been criticized in certain respects. His Book of Shadows is the foundation-stone of the Gardnerian form of modern Wicca, and also of its Alexandrian offshoot; and it has had considerable influence on many Traditional covens. Doreen Valiente, too, deserves every witch's gratitude; some of her contributions to the Book of Shadows have become its best-loved passages—the Charge, for instance, the unique and definitive statement of Wiccan philosophy. But for some reason, the rituals which the Book lays down for the Eight Sabbats are very sketchy indeed—nothing like as full and satisfying as the rest. The summary which Stewart gave to them in Chapter 7 of *What Witches Do* (see Bibliography) would seem to include everything which Gardner had to say on them. Anything else was left to the covens' imagination and inventiveness.

Some witches may feel that this is enough. Wicca is, after all,

---

2. There is a tiny Russian Orthodox community in Ireland, based on exiles from Russia; interestingly, "it has attracted quite a number of Irish converts, some of whom regard it as the Irish Church which existed from before the arrival of St Patrick to the years following Henry's invasion and the establishment of the links with Rome" (*Sunday Press*, Dublin, 12th March 1978).

a natural and spontaneous religion, in which every coven is a law to itself, and rigid forms are avoided. Nothing is quite the same for two Circles running—and quite right too, or Wicca would fossilize. So why not leave these sketchy Sabbat rituals as they are, use them as a starting-point and let each Sabbat take its own course? Everyone knows the 'feel' of the seasons . . .

We feel that there are two reasons why this is *not* enough. First, the other basic rituals—casting the Circle, Drawing Down the Moon, the Charge, the Legend of the Descent of the Goddess, and so on—*are* all substantial, and newcomers and old hands alike find them moving and satisfying. The flexibility which a good High Priestess and High Priest bring to them, and the planned or spontaneous embellishments which they add, merely enhance the basic rituals and keep them vivid and alive. If they had been sketchy to begin with, would ordinary people have been able to make so much of them?

Second, in our urban civilization it is unfortunately not true that everyone knows the 'feel' of the seasons, except very superficially. Even many country-dwellers, with their cars and electricity and television and standardized market-town (or even village) supermarkets, are remarkably well insulated from the gut-feeling of Nature. The archetypal knowledge of the physical and psychic tides of the year, which made such concepts as the fraternal rivalry of the Oak King and Holly King and their sacrificial mating with the Great Mother (to take just one example) perfectly comprehensible to our ancestors— concepts which, together with their symbolism, are so astonishingly widespread in time and space that they *must* be archetypal: this knowledge is virtually lost to modern consciousness.

Archetypes cannot be eradicated, any more than bones or nerves can; they are as much part of us. But they can become so deeply buried that it takes deliberate effort to re-establish healthy and fruitful communication with them.

Most people's awareness of the seasonal rhythms today is limited to such surface manifestations as Christmas cards, Easter eggs, sunbathing, autumn leaves and overcoats. And to be honest, the Book of Shadows' Sabbat rituals go very little deeper.

To return to ourselves. Ours is an Alexandrian coven—if we

must tie a label round our necks, for we are unsectarian by temperament and principle and prefer simply to call ourselves 'witches'. We have many Gardnerian and Traditional friends and regard their ways as just as valid as ours. We were initiated and trained by Alex and Maxine Sanders, founded our own coven in London at Yule 1970 and thereafter followed our own judgement (at one stage defying an order to disband the coven and return to Alex for 'further instruction'). We have seen ourselves referred to as 'reformed' Alexandrians—which has some truth, in that we have learned to sort out the undeniable wheat from the regrettable chaff. Other covens, and solo witches, have hived off from ours in the normal process of growth, and since we moved from crowded London to the fields and mountains of Ireland in April 1976 we have built up yet others; so our experience has been varied.

Our coven is organized on the customary Gardnerian/ Alexandrian lines; namely, it is based on the polarity of psychic femaleness and maleness. It consists, as far as possible, of 'working partnerships', each of one female and one male witch. Working partners may be a married couple, lovers, friends, brother and sister, parent and child; it does not matter whether or not their relationship is a sexual one. What matters is their psychic *gender*, so that in magical working they are two poles of a battery. The senior working partnership is, of course, that of the High Priestess and High Priest. She is *prima inter pares*, first among equals; the High Priest is her complementary equal (otherwise their 'battery' would produce no power), but she is the leader of the coven and he the 'Prince Consort'.

This question of the matriarchal emphasis in Wicca has been the cause of considerable argument, even among witches—with everything from cave paintings to Margaret Murray being used as ammunition in attempts to prove what used to be done, what is the 'true' tradition. Such evidence, honestly examined, is of course important—but we feel it is not the whole answer. More attention should be paid to the role of the Old Religion in today's conditions; in short, to what works best *now*, as well as to those factors which are timeless. And as we see it, the matriarchal emphasis is justified on both these counts.

First, the timeless aspect. Wicca, by its very nature, is concerned especially with the development and use of 'the gift of the Goddess'—the psychic and intuitive faculties—and to a rather lesser degree with 'the gift of the God'—the linear-logical, conscious faculties. Neither can function without the other, and the gift of the Goddess must be developed and exercised in both male and female witches. But the fact remains that, *on the whole*, woman has a flying start with the gift of the Goddess, just as man *on the whole* has a flying start with muscle. And within the Circle the High Priestess (though she calls upon her High Priest to invoke it) is the channel and representative of the Goddess.

This is not just Wiccan custom, it is a fact of Nature. "A woman," says Carl Jung, "can identify directly with the Earth Mother, but a man cannot (except in psychotic cases)." (*Collected Works, volume IX, part 1*, 2nd edition, para. 193.) On this point, Wiccan experience fully supports that of clinical psychology. If Wiccan emphasis is on the gift of the Goddess (supported and energized by the gift of the God), then in practice it must also be on the Priestess (supported and energized by the Priest). (For a deeper study of this magical relationship, read any of Dion Fortune's novels—especially *The Sea Priestess* and *Moon Magic*.)

Second, the 'now' aspect—the requirements of our present stage of evolution. A whole book could be written on this; here, we can only over-simplify history considerably—but without, we believe, distorting its basic truth. By and large, until three or four thousand years ago the human race lived (like other animals though at a much complex level) by 'the gift of the Goddess'; in psychological terms, human activity was dominated by the promptings of the subconscious mind, consciousness being still on the whole secondary. Society was generally matrilinear (acknowledging descent through the mother) and often also matriarchal (woman-governed), with the emphasis on the Goddess, the Priestess, the Queen, the Mother.[3] "Before

---

3. Ancient Egypt was a copybook example of the transition stage; it was matrilinear but patriarchal, both royalty and property passing strictly through the female line. All the male Pharaohs held the throne *because they were married to the heiress*: "The queen was queen by right of birth, the king was king by right of marriage" (Margaret Murray, *The Splendour that was Egypt*, p. 70), hence the Pharaonic habit of marrying sisters and daughters to retain the right to the throne. Matrilinear inheritance was the rule at all levels of society and

civilization sets in, the earth is one universal deity . . . a living creature; a female, because it receives the power of the sun, is animated thereby and made fertile. . . . The oldest and deepest element in any religion is the cult of the earth spirit in her many aspects." (John Michell, *The Earth Spirit*, p. 4.) To this should be added—certainly as mankind's awareness increased—the Queen of Heaven aspect too; for, to humanity in this phase, the Great Mother was the womb and nourisher of the whole cosmos, matter and spirit alike.[4]

We must emphasize that this interpretation is *not* a backstairs way of introducing any idea of 'female intellectual inferiority'. On the contrary, as Merlin Stone points out (*The Paradise Papers*, p. 210), the Goddess-worshipping cultures produced "inventions in methods of agriculture, medicine, architecture, metallurgy, wheeled vehicles, ceramics, textiles and written language"—in which women played a full part (sometimes, as with the introduction of agriculture, the leading one). It would be truer to say that the developing intellect was a tool for making the most of what was natural, instead of (as it became later) all too often for distorting or crushing it.

But the long climb to consciousness was accelerating—and suddenly (in terms of the evolutionary time-scale) the conscious mind was launched on its meteoric rise to dictatorship over mankind's affairs and environment. Inevitably, this was expressed in patriarchal monotheism—the rule of the God, the Priest, the King, the Father. (In the Mediterranean cradle of civilization, the carriers of this new outlook were the patri-

---

persisted to the very end; that was why first Julius Caesar and then Antony married Cleopatra, the last Pharaoh—it was the only way they could be acknowledged as rulers of Egypt. Octavius (Augustus Caesar) offered to marry her too, after Antony's defeat and death, but she preferred suicide (*ibid.*, pp. 70–71). Rome confronted the same principle a century later at the other end of its Empire, in Britain, when Roman flouting of it (whether clumsy or deliberate) provoked the furious revolt of the Celtic Iceni under Boudicca (Boadicea). (See Lethbridge's *Witches*, pp. 79–80.)

4. Kalderash Gypsies (one of the three main Romany groups) maintain that *O Del*, The (masculine) God, did not create the world. "The earth (*phu*), that is, the universe, existed before him; it always existed. 'It is the mother of all of us' (*amari De*) and is called *De Develeski*, the Divine Mother. In this one recognizes a trace of the primitive matriarchy." (Jean-Paul Clébert, *The Gypsies*, p. 134.)

linear, God-worshipping Indo-European peoples who conquered or infiltrated the indigenous matrilinear, Goddess-
worshipping cultures; for the history of the take-over, and its
effect on religion and the subsequent relationship between the
sexes, Ms Stone's *Paradise Papers*, quoted above, is well worth
reading.) It was a necessary, if bloodily tragic, stage in
mankind's evolution; and it involved, equally inevitably, a
certain shelving—often a vigorous Establishment suppression—of the free exercise of the gift of the Goddess.

This is over-simplification enough to make a historian's hair
stand on end, but food for thought. And here is more. That
stage of evolution is over. The development of the conscious
mind (certainly in the best examples available to mankind) has
reached its peak. Our next evolutionary task is to revive the gift
of the Goddess at full strength *and combine the two*—with
unimaginable prospects for the human race and the planet we
live on. God is not dead; he is a grass-widower, awaiting the
readmission of his exiled Consort. And if Wicca is to play its
part in this, a special emphasis *on that which is to be reawakened* is
a practical necessity, in order to restore the balance between the
two Gifts.[5]

For balance it is, and must be, which is why we emphasize
both the essential equality of man and woman in a Wiccan
working partnership *and* the advisability of the High Priestess's
being recognized as 'first among equals' in her own relationship with her High Priest and the coven—a delicate balance
with some partnerships, but our own experience (and our
observation of other covens) convinces us that it is worth
pursuing.

One might also point out that in this time of spiritual turmoil
and wide-spread religious re-assessment, Catholicism,

---

5. As this book was going to press, we read Annie Wilson's newly published
book *The Wise Virgin*. In her Section Four, "The Heart of the Matter", she
deals in depth with this question of the evolution of consciousness and has
some very perceptive things to say about its psychological, spiritual and sexual
(in the widest sense) implications. She, too, concludes that a new synthesis, of
excitingly creative potential, is not only possible but urgently necessary if we
in the West "are to balance our acute lopsidedness". This is very helpful
reading for a deeper understanding of the nature, function and relationship of
male and female.

Judaism, Islam and much of Protestanism still stubbornly cling to the male monopoly of priesthood as 'divinely ordained'; the Priestess is still banned, to the great spiritual impoverishment of mankind. This balance, too, Wicca can help to redress. And every active Wiccan Priestess knows from her own experience how great is the vacuum to be filled—indeed, there are times when it is difficult not to be overwhelmed by it (even, let it be whispered, times when priests and ministers of other religions come to her unofficially for help, frustrated by their own lack of female colleagues).

After that necessary digression—back to the structure of the coven.

The ideal of a coven consisting entirely of working partnerships is, of course, seldom achieved; there will always be one or two unpartnered members.

One woman member is appointed as the Maiden; she is in effect an assistant High Priestess for ritual purposes—though not necessarily in the sphere of leadership and authority. The role of the Maiden varies from coven to coven, but most find it useful to have one, to play a particular role in the rituals. (The Maiden usually—in our coven, anyway—has her own working partner just like any other coven member.)

In this book, we have assumed the above structure—High Priestess, High Priest, Maiden, some working partnerships and one or two unpartnered members.

As for the Sabbats—in our own coven we began, as one might expect, by taking the Book of Shadows as each one came up, applying a little on-the-spot inventiveness to the limited material it gave and letting it develop into a coven party. (Let us be quite clear about that, lest all this serious analysis mislead anybody: every Sabbat *should* develop into a party.) But over the years we began to find this inadequate. Eight good parties, each starting off with a bit of partly inherited and partly spontaneous ritual, were not enough to express the joy, mystery and magic of the turning year, or the ebb and flow of the psychic tides which underlie it. They were like eight little tunes, pleasant but separate, when what we really wanted was eight movements of one symphony.

So we began to delve and study, to seek out seasonal clues in everything from Robert Graves's *White Goddess* to Ovid's *Fasti*, from books on folklore customs to theories about stone circles, from Jungian psychology to weather lore. Archaeological holidays in Greece and Egypt, and fortunate professional visits to the Continent, helped to widen our horizons. Above all, perhaps, moving into the country, surrounded by plants, trees, crops, animals and weather of practical concern to us, brought us face-to-face with manifested Nature in our daily lives; her rhythms began to be truly our rhythms.

We tried to discover the yearly pattern behind all this and to apply what we learned to our Sabbat rituals. And as we did so, the Sabbats began to come to life for us.

We tried always to *extract* a pattern, not to *impose* one; and extracting it is not easy. It is a complex task, because Wicca[6] is an integral part of the Western pagan tradition; and the roots of that tradition spread wide, from the Norse lands to the Middle East and Egypt, from the steppes to the Atlantic seaboard. To emphasize one strand of the web (say the Celtic, the Norse or the Greek) and to use its particular forms and symbols, because you are in tune with them, is reasonable and even desirable; but to *isolate* that one strand, to attempt to reject the others as alien to it, is as unrealistic and doomed to failure as trying to

---

6. Like most modern witches, we call the Craft 'Wicca'. This has become a well-established, and much-loved, usage, and there is every reason why it should continue—but we might as well be honest and admit that it is in effect a *new* word, mistakenly derived. The Old English for 'witchcraft' was *wicca-craeft*, not *wicca*. *Wicca* meant 'a male witch' (feminine *wicce*, plural *wiccan*), from the verb *wiccian*, 'to bewitch, to practise witchcraft', which the *Oxford English Dictionary* says is "of obscure origin". For the OED, the trail seems to stop there; but Gardner's assertion that Wicca (or, as he spells it, Wica) means "the Craft of the Wise" is supported by Margaret Murray, who wrote the *Encyclopaedia Britannica* (1957) entry on Witchcraft. "The actual meaning of this word 'witch' is allied with 'wit', *to know*." Robert Graves (*The White Goddess*, p. 173), discussing the willow which in Greece was sacred to Hecate, says: "Its connexion with witches is so strong in Northern Europe that the words 'witch' and 'wicked' are derived from the same ancient word for willow, which also yields 'wicker'." To complete the picture, 'wizard' did mean 'a wise one', being derived from the Late Middle English *wys* or *wis*, 'wise'. But 'warlock', in the sense of 'a male witch', is Scottish Late Middle English and entirely derogatory; its root means 'traitor, enemy, devil'; and if the very few modern male witches who call themselves warlocks realized its origin, they would join the majority and share the title 'witch' with their sisters.

unscramble one parent's genes from a living offspring. The Old Religion, too, is a living organism. Its spirit is timeless, and the sap that runs in its veins does not change—but at any one time and place, it is at a particular stage of growth. You can put yourself in tune with that growth, encourage and contribute to it and influence its future; but you are asking for trouble and disappointment if you distort or misrepresent it.

We have already pointed out that the Eight Sabbats reflect two distinct themes, with different though interacting historical roots: the solar theme and the natural-fertility theme. They are no longer separable, but each must be understood if both are to be fitted into our 'symphony'.

It seemed to us that a key to this understanding was to recognize that two concepts of the God-figure were involved. The Goddess is always there; she changes her aspect (both in her fecundity cycle as the Earth Mother and in her lunar phases as the Queen of Heaven), but she is ever-present. But the God, in both concepts, dies and is reborn.

This is fundamental. The concept of a sacrificed and resurrected God is found everywhere, back to the dimmest hints of prehistory; Osiris, Tammuz, Dionysos, Balder and Christ are only some of his later forms. But you will search in vain throughout the history of religion for a sacrificed and resurrected Goddess—seasonally lost to view, perhaps, like Persephone, but sacrificed, never. Such a concept would be religiously, psychologically and naturally unthinkable.[7]

Let us look, then, at these two God-themes.

The Sun-God figure, which dominates the Lesser Sabbats of solstices and equinoxes, is comparatively simple; his cycle can be observed even through the window of a high-rise flat. He dies and is reborn at Yule; begins to make his young maturity felt, and to impregnate Mother Earth with it, around the Spring

---

7. We have come across only one apparent exception to this rule. On p. 468 of *The Golden Bough* Frazer says: "In Greece the great goddess Artemis herself appears to have been annually hanged in effigy in her sacred grove of Condylea among the Arcadian hills, and there accordingly she went by the name of the Hanged One." But Frazer missed the point. 'Hanged Artemis' is no sacrifice—she is an aspect of the Spider Goddess Arachne/Ariadne/Arianrhod/ (Aradia?), who descends to aid us on her magic thread, and whose spiral web is the key to rebirth. (See James Vogh, *The Thirteenth Zodiac*.)

Equinox; blazes at the peak of his glory at Midsummer; resigns himself to waning power, and waning influence on the Great Mother, around the Autumn Equinox; and again faces Yuletide death and rebirth.

The natural-fertility theme is more complex; it involves *two* God-figures—the God of the Waxing Year (who appears time and again in mythology as the Oak King)⁸ and the God of the Waning Year (the Holly King). They are the light and dark twins, each the other's 'other self', eternal rivals eternally conquering and succeeding each other. They compete eternally for the favour of the Great Mother; and each, at the peak of his half-yearly reign, is sacrificially mated with her, dies in her embrace and is resurrected to complete his reign.

'Light and dark' do not mean 'good and evil'; they mean the expansive and contractive phases of the yearly cycle, each as necessary as the other. From the creative tension between the two of them, and between them on the one hand and the Goddess on the other, life is generated.

This theme in fact overflows into the Lesser Sabbats of Yule and Midsummer. At Yule the Holly King ends his reign and falls to the Oak King; at Midsummer the Oak King in turn is ousted by the Holly King.

This is a book of suggested rituals, not a work of detailed historical analysis; so it is not the place to explain in depth just how we extracted the above pattern. But we believe that anyone who studies Western mythology with an open mind will inevitably reach the same general conclusions; and most witches will probably recognize the pattern already.

(Some of them may quite reasonably ask: "Where does our Horned God fit into this?" The Horned God is a natural-fertility figure; the roots of his symbolism go back to totemic and hunting epochs. He is Oak King *and* Holly King, the complementary twins seen as one complete entity. We would suggest that Oak King and Holly King are a subtlety which developed in amplification of the Horned God concept as vegetation became more important to man. They did not abolish him— they merely increased our understanding of him.)

---

8. Also doubtless relatable to the Green Man or Foliate Mask whose carved features appear in so many old churches.

At the beginning of each Section of this book, we give more details of the background to each Sabbat and explain how we have used it to devise our ritual.

But to help to make the overall pattern clearer, we have tried to summarize it in the diagram on p. 26. It *is* only a summary, but we have found it helpful, and we hope that other people will too.

One or two comments on it are necessary. First, the 'aspects of the Goddess'—Birth, Initiation, Consummation, Repose and Death—are those suggested in Graves's *White Goddess*. (Robert Graves's writings, and those of Doreen Valiente, have been of more help to us in our research than perhaps any others.) It should be emphasized again that these do not mean the birth and death of the Goddess herself (an unthinkable concept, as we have pointed out) but the face which she shows to the God and to her worshippers as the year turns. She does not *undergo* the experiences so much as *preside* over them.

Second, the placing of the sacrificial mating and rebirth of Oak King and Holly King, at Bealtaine and Lughnasadh respectively, may seem a little arbitrary. Because this cycle is a fertility one, the actual spacing of its rhythm varies from region to region; naturally so, because the calendars of a Scottish Highland croft and an Italian vineyard (for example) do not keep exact step with each other. The two sacrifices appear at various times in the Spring and Autumn; so in devising a coherent cycle of Sabbats, a choice had to be made. Bealtaine seemed the obvious choice for the Oak King's mating; but the Holly King's (even confining ourselves to the Greater Sabbats, as seemed fitting) could be either Lughnasadh or Samhain—at both of which traces of it are to be found. One reason why we settled for Lughnasadh was that Samhain (Hallowe'en) is already so charged with meaning and tradition that to incorporate the Holly King's sacrifice, mating and rebirth in its ritual would overload it to the point of confusion. Each Sabbat, however complex its overtones, should have a central theme and a clear message. Again, the Holly King's sacrifice is also that of the Corn King—a stubbornly indestructible folk-theme, as many symbolic customs indicate;[9] and Lughnasadh, not

9. Read *Harvest Home* by Thomas Tryon—a terrifying but discerning novel, now made into a very good film.

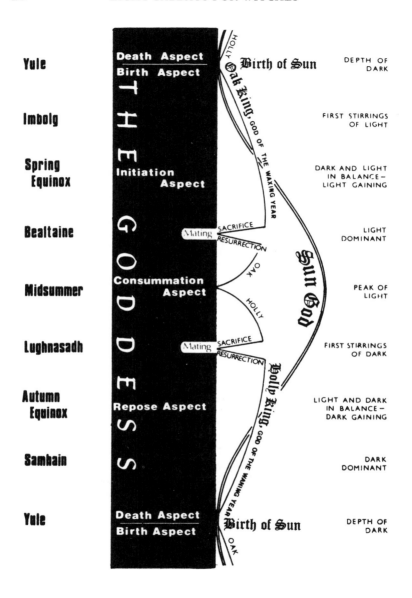

Samhain, marks the harvest. Finally, we have tried wherever possible to include in our suggested rituals the essentials of the Book of Shadows rites; and that for Lughnasadh, cryptic though it is, does point to this interpretation. It is the only occasion when the High Priestess invokes the Goddess into herself, instead of the High Priest doing it for her, a hint perhaps that at this Sabbat she is even more powerfully in command, and the Sacrificial God even more vulnerable? It seemed so to us.

In deciding how to cast male witches for the roles of Sun God, Oak King and Holly King, we were governed by two considerations: (1) that the High Priestess, as representative of the Goddess, has only one 'consort'—her working partner, the High Priest—and that any ritual which symbolizes her mating must be with him; and (2) that it is not practicable or desirable for the High Priest to finish any ritual symbolically 'dead', since he is the male leader of the coven under the High Priestess and must, so to speak, be restored to availability in the course of the ritual.

At Bealtaine and Lughnasadh, therefore—the two rites of sacrificial mating and rebirth—we have the High Priest enacting the Oak King and Holly King, respectively. In each case the ritual implies his mating with the Great Mother, and his 'death'; and before the ritual drama ends, he is reborn. The Sun God is not enacted, as such, at these Sabbats.

At Midsummer and Yule, however, all three God-aspects are involved. At Midsummer, the Sun God is at the peak of his power, and the Holly King 'slays' the Oak King. At Yule, the Sun God undergoes death and rebirth, and the Oak King in turn 'slays' the Holly King. On these two occasions, the Goddess does not mate, she presides; and at Yule, in addition, she gives birth to the renewed Sun God. So for these two, we have the High Priest enacting the Sun God, while the Oak King and Holly King are ritually chosen by lot (unless the High Priestess prefers to nominate them) and crowned for their roles by the Maiden. We have been careful to include in each ritual the formal release of the actor of the slain King from his role (thus restoring him to his place in the coven for the rest of the Sabbat), and also an explanation of what happens to the spirit of the slain King during his coming half-year of eclipse.

This book is about the Sabbats. But Esbats (non-Festival meetings) and Sabbats have one thing in common: they are all held within a Magic Circle, which is ritually set up, or 'cast', at the beginning of the meeting and ritually dispersed, or 'banished', at the end. These opening and closing rituals, even within the Gardnerian/Alexandrian tradition, tend to vary in detail from coven to coven and may also vary from occasion to occasion in the same coven, according to the work to be done and the High Priestess's intuitive or conscious decision. Nevertheless, each coven has its basic opening and closing rituals, however flexible; and it will use these at Esbats and Sabbats alike. Usually the opening ritual includes, in addition to the actual casting of the Circle, 'Drawing Down the Moon' (invocation of the spirit of the Goddess into the High Priestess by the High Priest) and the recital of the Charge (the traditional address of the Goddess to her followers).

Another common feature of all eight Sabbats, as laid down by the Book of Shadows, is the Great Rite, the ritual of male-female polarity enacted by the High Priestess and High Priest.

Since this book consists of *our* detailed suggestions for the eight Sabbat rituals, it would therefore be incomplete if we did not also present *our* particular way of carrying out the Opening Ritual, the Great Rite and the Closing Ritual. So we have included them as Sections I, II and III. We do not suggest that ours are 'better' than other covens'; but they are at least in the same style as our suggested Sabbat rituals, thus putting the latter in context instead of leaving them topless and tailless. Also, we hope that some covens will find it useful to have a form for the symbolic Great Rite, which the Book of Shadows fails to give.

We hope it is no longer necessary at this late stage to defend ourselves against the charge of 'betraying secrets' by publishing our versions of the Opening, Closing and Great Rite rituals. The basic Gardnerian rituals have been 'in the public domain' for many years now; and so many versions of these particular three (some garbled, and at least one—by Peter Haining—shamelessly black) have been published, that we make no apology for offering what we feel to be coherent and workable ones.

Besides, with the publication of Doreen Valiente's *Witchcraft for Tomorrow*, the Wiccan situation has changed. On the principle that 'you have a right to be a pagan if you want to be', she has decided "to write a book which will put witchcraft within the reach of all" (and no one is better qualified to take that decision than the co-author of the Book of Shadows). *Witchcraft for Tomorrow* includes a *Liber Umbrarum*, her completely new and very simple Book of Shadows for people who want to initiate themselves and organize their own covens. Already, like Gardner before her, she is being both praised and attacked for her initiative. For ourselves, we welcome it wholeheartedly. Since Stewart published *What Witches Do*, nine years ago, we have been (and still are) flooded with letters from people asking to be put in touch with a coven in their locality. Most of them we have been unable to help, especially as they are scattered all round the world. In future we shall refer them to *Witchcraft for Tomorrow*. The need is genuine, widespread and growing; and to leave it unsatisfied for reasons of alleged 'secrecy' is negative and unrealistic.

Interestingly, what Doreen Valiente has done for Gardnerian Wicca in *Witchcraft for Tomorrow*, Raymond Buckland has also done for another tradition, Saxon Wicca, in *The Tree, The Complete Book of Saxon Witchcraft* (see Bibliography). That, too, includes a simple but comprehensive Book of Shadows and procedures for self-initiation and the founding of your own coven. We found many of the rituals in *The Tree* admirable, though we were less happy about its eight Festival rites, which are even scantier than those in the Gardnerian Book of Shadows, and amount to little more than brief spoken declamations; they are based on the idea that the Goddess rules the summer, from Bealtaine to Samhain, and the God the winter, from Samhain to Bealtaine—a concept to which we cannot attune ourselves. Persephone, who withdraws to the underworld in winter, is only one aspect of the Goddess—a fact which her legend emphasizes by making her the *daughter* of the Great Mother.

However, to each his own; it is presumptuous to be too dogmatic, from the outside, about other traditions of the Craft. What matters is that anyone who wants to follow the Wiccan path but cannot get in touch with an established coven, now has *two* valid Wiccan traditions open to him in published form. What he makes of them depends on his own sincerity and determination—but that would be equally true if he joined an established coven in the normal way.

Referring again to *What Witches Do*, there is one apology Stewart *would* like to make. When he wrote it, as a first-year witch, he included material which he then understood to be either traditional or originating from his teachers. He now knows that much of it was in fact written for Gardner by Doreen Valiente. She has been kind enough to say: "I of course accept that you did not know this when you published them; how could you?" So we are glad, this time round, to have the opportunity to put the record straight. And we are grateful to her for having read this manuscript before publication, at our request, to make sure that we have neither quoted her without acknowledgement nor misquoted her. (A similar apology, by the way, to the shade of the late Franz Bardon.)

Doreen's help has given us another reason for including the Opening, Great Rite and Closing rituals as well as the eight Festivals; it has enabled us to give definitive answers to most (we hope) of the questions that people have been asking for the past quarter-century about the sources of the various elements in the Book of Shadows (or at least those sections of it within the scope of this book) and the circumstances of its compiling. We believe it is time for this to be done. The confusion and mis-representation (sometimes innocent, sometimes deliberate) has gone on long enough, leading even such a distinguished occult historian as our friend Francis King to arrive at mistaken—if understandable—conclusions about it.

To clarify sources and origins is *not* to 'take the mystery out of the Mysteries'. The Mysteries cannot, by their nature, ever be fully described in words; they can only be experienced. But they can be invoked and activated by effective ritual. One must never confuse the words and actions of ritual with the Mystery itself. The ritual is not the Mystery—it is a way of contacting and experiencing it. To plead 'safeguarding the Mysteries' as an excuse for falsifying history and concealing plagiarism is wrong, and a disservice both to the Mysteries themselves and to those whom you teach. That includes, for example, claiming to have copied the Book of Shadows from your grandmother many years before it was in fact compiled, or dictating other teachers' work to trusting students as your own.

The rituals in this book are given as for indoor working, but they can all be easily adapted for outdoor working where this is happily possible. For example, candles can be lit in lanterns or jars, and bonfires lit where suitable and safe. (If you work skyclad—that is, naked—a bonfire helps!)

Because each of these rituals is performed only once a year, obviously no one is going to know them by heart in the way that Esbat rituals are known. So the declamations at least will be read from the script. Eyesight varies, so it is up to the person concerned whether, and when, to pick up one of the altar candles to read by—or, if he or she needs both hands, to call another witch to hold it. To save repetition, we have not referred to this except where experience has taught us it is particularly necessary; for example, when the High Priestess drapes a veil over her face (at which times, incidentally, provided the veil is long enough, she should hold the script *inside* it).

We have found it a great help, wherever possible, to have a brief rehearsal beforehand. It need take only five minutes, before the Circle is cast. No declamations are read; all that is required is for the High Priest or High Priestess to have the script in his or her hand, and to run quickly through the sequence, explaining, "Then I do this, and you do that, while she stands over there . . ." and so on, to make sure that everybody has the basic sequence and any key movements clear. This does not detract from the ritual itself; in fact, it makes it run much more smoothly when the time comes and avoids excessive 'sheepdogging' or worrying about possible mistakes.

We have added the third part of the book—"Birth, Marriage and Death"—because, again, we feel there is a need for it. Alongside the universal rhythm of the seasons, runs the rhythm of our individual lives. Every religion feels the need for a sacramental acknowledgement of the milestones in those lives—the welcoming of new children, the joining together of man and wife, the solemn valediction to dead friends. Wicca is no exception, yet the Gardnerian Book of Shadows offers no ritual for any of them. So we give our own versions of the

Wiccaning, Handfasting and Requiem, in the hope that other people may find them useful.

Postscript to 1985 Reprint

Since this book was published, our later book *The Witches' Way* has appeared (Robert Hale Ltd., 1984). As well as giving an overall survey of Craft practice, it completes the task we began here—of establishing (again with Doreen Valiente's help) the exact form and wording of Gardner's rituals, from his original manuscripts in Doreen's possession. For example, it includes his own fuller version of the Great Rite, and all the non-ritual passages of his Book of Shadows.

We hope that readers will find it a helpful complementary volume to the present one.

This book was written in Ballycroy, Co. Mayo, on Ireland's Atlantic coast. But since then, our work has required us to move closer to Dublin. We can be written to at the address below.

JANET FARRAR
STEWART FARRAR

Barfordstown Lodge,
Kells,
Co. Meath, Ireland.

Bealtaine 1985

The Frame

I   The Opening Ritual

With this basic Wiccan ritual, we set up our Temple—our place of worship and magical working. It may be in a living-room with the furniture pushed back; it may be, if we are lucky enough to have one, in a room which is set aside for the purpose and used for no other; it may be, weather and privacy permitting, in the open air. But wherever we hold our Sabbat, this (in one form or another) is its essential beginning, just as the Closing Ritual given in Section III is its essential ending.

The Opening Ritual is the same for each of the Sabbats; where there are differences of detail, or of the furnishing or decorating of the Temple, these will be indicated at the beginning of each Sabbat Section.

The Preparation

The Circle area is cleared and an altar set up at the Northern point of its circumference. (See Plate 1.) This altar may be a small table (a coffee-table is ideal) or merely a cloth laid on the floor. Arranged on the altar are:

> the pentacle in the centre
> the North candle, behind the pentacle
> a pair of altar candles, one at each side
> the chalice of red wine or of mead
> the wand
> the scourge of silken cords
> a small bowl of water
> a small bowl with a little salt in it
> the cords (red, white and blue, nine feet long each)
> the white-handled knife
> each witch's individual athame (black-handled knife)
> the incense-burner
> a small hand-bell
> a dish of cakes or biscuits
> the sword, on the floor in front of the altar, or on the altar itself.

A supply of the chosen incense, and matches or a cigarette-lighter, should be handy by the altar. (We find a taper useful for carrying flame from candle to candle.)

A candle is placed at each of the East, South and West points of the circumference of the Circle, completing the four 'elemental' candles which must burn throughout the ritual. (The elemental placings are East, Air; South, Fire; West, Water; and North, Earth.)

Music should be available. For ourselves, we have built up a small library of C-120 cassettes of suitable music, transferred from discs or other cassettes, with each piece of music repeated as often as necessary to fill the whole sixty minutes of one track. Cassettes are ideal, because they can be played on anything from stereo hi-fi, if your living-room has it, to a portable player if you are meeting elsewhere. It is a good idea to adjust the volume to suit the loudest passages *before* the ritual, otherwise you may be unexpectedly deafened and have to fiddle with it at an inappropriate moment.

Make sure the room is warm enough well in advance—
especially if, like ourselves and most Gardnerian/Alexandrian
covens, you normally work skyclad.

Only one place outside the Circle itself needs to be clear—the
North-East quadrant, because the coven stands there to begin
with, waiting for the High Priestess to admit them.

Take the phone off the hook, light the incense and the six
candles, start the music, and you are ready to begin.

The Ritual

The High Priestess and High Priest kneel before the altar, with
him to her right. The rest of the coven stand outside the
North-East quadrant of the Circle.

The High Priestess puts the bowl of water on the pentacle,
puts the point of her athame in the water (see Plate 2) and
says:

"*I exorcise thee, O creature of water, that thou cast out from thee
all the impurities and uncleanliness of the spirits of the world of
phantasm; in the names of Cernunnos and Aradia.*" (Or whatever
God and Goddess names the coven uses.)[1]

She lays down her athame and holds up the bowl of water in
both hands. The High Priest puts the bowl of salt on the
pentacle, puts the tip of his athame in the salt and says:

"*Blessings be upon this creature of salt; let all malignity and
hindrance be cast forth hencefrom, and let all good enter herein;
wherefore do I bless thee, that thou mayest aid me, in the names of
Cernunnos and Aradia.*"[1]

He lays down his athame and pours the salt into the bowl of
water which the High Priestess is holding up. They then both

---

1. Both these consecrations are very loosely based on those in *The Key of
Solomon*, a mediaeval grimoire, or 'grammar', of magical practice translated
and edited by MacGregor Mathers from manuscripts in the British Museum
and published in 1888. (See Bibliography under Mathers.) The wording for
the consecration of magical tools in Gardner's Book of Shadows also follows
(and rather more closely) that in *The Key of Solomon*. That these were
Gardner's own borrowings, rather than part of the traditional material he
obtained from the New Forest coven which initiated him, is suggested by the
fact that their English corresponds to that of Mathers, instead of deriving
independently from the original Latin. There is no harm in that; like most of
Gardner's borrowings, they suit their purpose admirably.

put down their bowls on the altar, and the High Priest leaves the Circle to stand with the coven.

The High Priestess draws the Circle with the sword, leaving a gateway in the North-East (by raising her sword higher than the heads of the coven as she passes them). She proceeds deosil (clockwise)[2] from North to North, saying as she goes:

"I conjure thee, O Circle of Power, that thou beest a meeting-place of love and joy and truth; a shield against all wickedness and evil; a boundary between the world of men and the realms of the Mighty Ones; a rampart and protection that shall preserve and contain the power that we shall raise within thee. Wherefore do I bless thee and consecrate thee, in the names of Cernunnos and Aradia."

She then lays down the sword and admits the High Priest to the Circle with a kiss, spinning with him deosil. The High Priest admits a woman in the same way; that woman admits a man; and so on, till all the coven are in the Circle.

The High Priestess picks up the sword and closes the gateway, by drawing that part of the Circle in the same way as she did the rest of it.[3]

---

2. All magical movements involving rotation or circling are normally made clockwise, 'the way of the Sun'. This is known as 'deosil', from the Gaelic (Irish *deiseal*, Scottish *deiseil*, both pronounced approximately 'jesh'l') meaning 'to the right' or 'to the South'. (In Irish one says *'Deiseal'*—'May it go right'—when a friend sneezes.) An anti-clockwise movement is known as 'widdershins' (Middle High German *widersinnes*, 'in a contrary direction') or 'tuathal' (Irish *tuathal* pronounced 'twa-h'l', Scottish *tuaitheal* pronounced 'twa-y'l') meaning 'to the left, to the North, in a wrong direction'. A widdershins magical movement is considered black or malevolent, *unless* it has a precise symbolic meaning such as an attempt to regress in time, or a return to the source preparatory to rebirth; in such cases it is always in due course 'unwound' by a deosil movement—much as a Scottish Highlander begins a sword dance *tuaitheal*, because it is a war-dance, and ends it *deiseil* to symbolize victory. (See pp. 118, 134 and 169 for examples in our rituals.) We would be interested to hear from witches in the southern hemisphere (where of course the Sun moves anti-clockwise) about their customs in ritual movements, orientation of the elements and placing of the altar.

3. Normally, no one leaves or enters the Circle between the casting and banishing rituals; but if it should be necessary, a gateway must be opened by a ritual widdershins (anti-clockwise) sweep of the athame and closed immediately after use by a deosil (clockwise) sweep. (Sword and athame are ritually interchangeable.) See, for example, p. 53.

The High Priestess then names three witches to strengthen the Circle (which she has already established in the Earth element) with the elements of Water, Air and Fire.

The first witch carries the bowl of consecrated water round the Circle, deosil from North to North, sprinkling the perimeter as he/she goes. Then he/she sprinkles each member of the coven in turn. If it is a man, he ends by sprinkling the High Priestess, who then sprinkles him; if it is a woman, she ends by sprinkling the High Priest, who then sprinkles her. The water-carrier then replaces the bowl on the altar.

The second witch carries the smoking incense-burner round the perimeter, deosil from North to North, and replaces it on the altar.

The third witch carries one of the altar candles round the perimeter, deosil from North to North, and replaces it on the altar.

All the coven then pick up their athames and face the East, with the High Priestess and High Priest in front (he standing to her right). The High Priestess says:

"Ye Lords of the Watchtowers of the East, ye Lords of Air; I do summon, stir and call you up, to witness our rites and to guard the Circle."

As she speaks, she draws the Invoking Pentagram of Earth with her athame in the air in front of her, thus:[1]

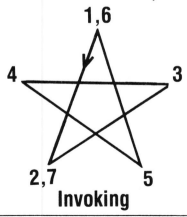

1,6

4   **3**

2,7   **5**

Invoking

---

4. This Watchtowers ritual is obviously based on the Golden Dawn's "Lesser Ritual of the Pentagram" (see Israel Regardie's *Golden Dawn*, volume I, pp.

After drawing the Pentagram, she kisses her athame blade and lays it on her heart for a second or two.

The High Priest and the rest of the coven copy all these gestures with their own athames; any who are without athames use their right forefingers.

The High Priestess and coven then face the South and repeat the summoning; this time it is to "*Ye Lords of the Watchtowers of the South, ye Lords of Fire . . .*".

They then face the West, where the summoning is to "*Ye Lords of the Watchtowers of the West, ye Lords of Water, ye Lords of Death and of Initiation . . .*".

They then face the North, where the summoning is longer; the High Priestess says:

"*Ye Lords of the Watchtowers of the North, ye Lords of Earth; Boreas, thou guardian of the Northern portals; thou powerful God, thou gentle Goddess; we do summon, stir and call you up, to witness our rites and to guard the Circle.*"

All the coven replace their athames on the altar, and all but the High Priestess and High Priest go to the South of the Circle, where they stand facing towards the altar.

The High Priest now proceeds to 'draw down the Moon' on the High Priestess. She stands with her back to the altar, with the wand in her right hand and the scourge in her left, held against her breasts in the 'Osiris position'—the two shafts grasped in her clenched fists, her wrists crossed, and the shafts crossed again above them. (See Plate 10.) He kneels before her.

The High Priest gives the High Priestess the Fivefold Kiss, kissing her on the right foot, left foot, right knee, left knee, womb, right breast, left breast and lips. (When he reaches the womb, she opens her arms to the 'blessing position'.) As he does so, he says:

"*Blessed be thy feet, that have brought thee in these ways.*
Blessed be thy knees, that shall kneel at the sacred altar.
Blessed be thy womb,[5] *without which we would not be.*

106–7 and, for more complex material on the Invoking and Banishing Pentagrams, volume III, pp. 9–19). Incidentally, the Golden Dawn, and many witches, end the Pentagrams by merely returning to the starting-point—i.e., omitting the sixth 'sealing' stroke. As always, it is a matter of what 'feels right' to you.

5. When a woman gives the Fivefold Kiss to a man (as at the Imbolg Sabbat) she says 'phallus' instead of 'womb', kissing him just above the pubic hair; and 'breast, formed in strength' instead of 'breasts, formed in beauty'.

Blessed be thy breasts, formed in beauty.[5]
Blessed be thy lips, that shall utter the Sacred Names."

For the kiss on the lips, they embrace, length-to-length, with their feet touching each other's.

The High Priest kneels again before the High Priestess, who resumes the 'blessing position', but with her right foot slightly forward. The High Priest invokes:

"I invoke thee and call upon thee, Mighty Mother of us all, bringer of all fruitfulness; by seed and root, by bud and stem, by leaf and flower and fruit, by life and love do I invoke thee to descend upon the body of this thy servant and priestess."

During this invocation he touches her with his right forefinger on her right breast, left breast and womb; the same three again; and finally the right breast. Still kneeling, he then spreads his arms outwards and downwards, with the palms forward, and says:[6]

> *"Hail, Aradia! From the Amalthean Horn*
> *Pour forth thy store of love; I lowly bend*
> *Before thee, I adore thee to the end,*
> *With loving sacrifice thy shrine adorn.*
> *Thy foot is to my lip . . ."*

He kisses her right foot and continues:

> *". . . my prayer upborne*
> *Upon the rising incense-smoke; then spend*
> *Thine ancient love, O Mighty One, descend*
> *To aid me, who without thee am forlorn."*

He then stands up and takes a pace backwards, still facing the High Priestess.

The High Priestess draws the Invoking Pentagram of Earth in the air in front of him with the wand, saying:[7]

> *"Of the Mother darksome and divine*
> *Mine the scourge, and mine the kiss;*

---

6. From a poem by Aleister Crowley, originally addressed to Tyche, Goddess of Fortune. Adapted for Craft use by Gardner, who was very fond of it.
7. From Doreen Valiente's rhymed version of the Charge.

The five-point star of love and bliss—
Here I charge you, in this sign."

With this, Drawing Down the Moon is complete; the next stage is the Charge. The High Priestess lays down the wand and scourge on the altar, and she and the High Priest face the coven, with him on her left. The High Priest says:

"Listen to the words of the Great Mother; she who of old was also called among men Artemis, Astarte, Athene, Dione, Melusine, Aphrodite, Cerridwen, Dana, Arianrhod, Isis, Bride,[9] and by many other names." [10]

The High Priestess says:

"Whenever ye have need of any thing, once in the month, and

---

8. The history of the Charge is as follows. Gardner drafted a first version, very similar to the one we give here down to "all in my praise" (this opening passage being adapted from the Tuscan witches' rituals recorded in Leland's *Aradia: the Gospel of the Witches*) followed by some voluptuously-worded extracts from Aleister Crowley. Doreen Valiente tells us she "felt that this was not really suitable for the Old Craft of the Wise, however beautiful the words might be or how much one might agree with what they said; so I wrote a version of the Charge in verse, keeping the words from *Aradia*, because these are traditional." This verse version began "Mother darksome and divine . . .", and its first stanza is still used as the High Priestess's response to the Drawing Down of the Moon. But most people seemed to prefer a prose Charge, so she wrote the final prose version we give here; it still contains one or two Crowley phrases ("Keep pure your highest ideal", for example, is from his essay *The Law of Liberty*, and "Nor do I demand (aught in) sacrifice" is from *The Book of the Law*) but she has integrated the whole to give us the best-loved declamation in today's Craft. It might be called a Wiccan Credo. Our version has one or two tiny differences from Doreen's (such as "witches" for "witcheries") but we have let them stand, with apologies to her.

9. Pronounced 'Breed'. If you have a local Goddess-name, by all means add it to the list. While we lived in County Wexford, we used to add Carman, a Wexford goddess (or heroine or villainess, according to your version) who gave the county and town their Gaelic name of Loch Garman (Loch gCarman).

10. In the Book of Shadows, another sentence follows here: "At her altars the youth of Lacedaemon in Sparta made due sacrifice." The sentence originated from Gardner, not Valiente. Like many covens, we omit it. The Spartan sacrifice, though it has been variously described, was certainly a gruesome business (see for example Robert Graves's *Greek Myths*, para 116.4) and out of keeping with the Charge's later statement "Nor do I demand sacrifice". By the way, the sentence is also inaccurately worded; Sparta was in Lacedaemon, not Lacedaemon in Sparta.

better it be when the moon is full, then shall ye assemble in some secret place and adore the spirit of me, who am Queen of all witches. There shall ye assemble, ye who are fain to learn all sorcery, yet have not won its deepest secrets; to these will I teach things that are yet unknown. And ye shall be free from slavery; and as a sign that ye be really free, ye shall be naked in your rites; and ye shall dance, sing, feast, make music and love, all in my praise. For mine is the ecstasy of the spirit, and mine also is joy on earth; for my law is love unto all beings. Keep pure your highest ideal; strive ever towards it; let naught stop you or turn you aside. For mine is the secret door which opens upon the Land of Youth, and mine is the cup of the wine of life, and the Cauldron of Cerridwen, which is the Holy Grail of immortality. I am the gracious Goddess, who gives the gift of joy unto the heart of man. Upon earth, I give the knowledge of the spirit eternal; and beyond death, I give peace, and freedom, and reunion with those who have gone before. Nor do I demand sacrifice; for behold, I am the Mother of all living, and my love is poured out upon the earth."

The High Priest says:

"Hear ye the words of the Star Goddess; she in the dust of whose feet are the hosts of heaven, and whose body encircles the universe."

The High Priestess says:

"I who am the beauty of the green earth, and the white Moon among the stars, and the mystery of the waters, and the desire of the heart of man, call unto thy soul. Arise, and come unto me. For I am the soul of nature, who gives life to the universe. From me all things proceed, and unto me all things must return; and before my face, beloved of Gods and of men, let thine innermost divine self be enfolded in the rapture of the infinite. Let my worship be within the heart that rejoiceth; for behold, all acts of love and pleasure are my rituals. And therefore let there be beauty and strength, power and compassion, honour and humility, mirth and reverence within you. And thou who thinkest to seek for me, know thy seeking and yearning shall avail thee not unless thou knowest the mystery; that if that which thou seekest thou findest not within thee, thou wilt never find it without thee. For behold, I have been with thee from the beginning; and I am that which is attained at the end of desire."

This is the end of the Charge.

The High Priest, still facing the coven, raises his arms wide and says:[11]

> *"Bagahi laca bachahé*
> *Lamac cahi achabahé*
> *Karrelyos*
> *Lamac lamec bachalyos*
> *Cabahagi sabalyos*
> *Baryolas*
> *Lagozatha cabyolas*
> *Samahac et famyolas*
> *Harrahya!"*

The High Priestess and the coven repeat "Harrahya!"

The High Priest and the High Priestess then turn to face the altar with their arms raised, their hands giving the 'Horned God' salute (forefinger and little finger straight, thumb and middle fingers folded into palm). The High Priest says:[12]

> *"Great God Cernunnos, return to earth again!*
> *Come at my call and show thyself to men.*
> *Shepherd of Goats, upon the wild hill's way,*
> *Lead thy lost flock from darkness unto day.*
> *Forgotten are the ways of sleep and night—*
> *Men seek for them, whose eyes have lost the light.*
> *Open the door, the door that hath no key,*
> *The door of dreams, whereby men come to thee.*
> *Shepherd of Goats, O answer unto me!"*

The High Priest and High Priestess say together:[13]

> *"Akhera goiti—akhera beiti!"*

—lowering their hands on the second phrase.

The High Priestess, followed by the High Priest, then leads the coven into the Witches' Rune—a ring dance deosil, facing inwards and holding hands (left palms upwards, right palms

---

11. This strange incantation, first known to have appeared in a thirteenth-century French play, is traditional in witchcraft. Its meaning is unknown—though Michael Harrison in *The Roots of Witchcraft* makes out an interesting case for its being a corruption of Basque, and a Samhain rallying-call.

12. This is the Invocation to Pan from Chapter XIII of *Moon Magic* by Dion Fortune, with the coven's God-name substituted for that of Pan.

13. This is an old Basque witches' incantation, meaning 'The he-goat above—the he-goat below'. We found it in Michael Harrison's *The Roots of Witchcraft*, liked it and adopted it.

downwards), men and women alternately as far as possible. The High Priestess sets the pace—and may sometimes let go of the hand of the man in front of her, and weave the coven after her, in and out like a snake. However complex her weaving, no one must let go, but all must keep moving, still hand-in-hand, till the line unravels itself. As the ring-dance proceeds, the whole coven chants:[14]

> *"Eko, Eko, Azarak,*
> *Eko, Eko, Zomelak,*   (repeated three times)
> *Eko, Eko, Cernunnos*
> *Eko, Eko, Aradia!*
> *Darksome night and shining moon,*
> *East, then South, then West, then North;*
> *Hearken to the Witches' Rune—*
> *Here we come to call ye forth!*
> *Earth and water, air and fire,*
> *Wand and pentacle and sword,*
> *Work ye unto our desire,*
> *Hearken ye unto our word!*
> *Cords and censer, scourge and knife,*
> *Powers of the witch's blade—*
> *Waken all ye into life,*
> *Come ye as the charm is made!*

---

14. This chant, the "Witches' Rune", was written by Doreen Valiente and Gerald Gardner together. The *"Eko, Eko"* lines (to which covens usually insert their own God and Goddess names in lines 3 and 4) were not part of their original Rune; she tells us: "We used to use them as a preface to the old chant *'Bagabi lacha bachabe'* " (to which Michael Harrison also attributes them) "but I don't think they were originally a part of this chant either, they were part of another old chant. Writing from memory, it went something like this:

> *Eko Eko Azarak*
> *Eko Eko Zomelak*
> *Zod ru koz e zod ru koo*
> *Zod ru goz e goo ru moo*
> *Eeo Eeo hoo hoo hoo!*

No, I don't know what they meant! But I think somehow that 'Azarak' and 'Zomelak' are God-names." She adds: "There's no reason why these words shouldn't be used as you have used them." We give here the version to which we, and many other covens, have become accustomed; the only differences are that the original has "I, my" instead of "we, our", and has *"East, then South and West and North"* and *"In the earth and air and sea, By the light of moon or sun"*,

Queen of heaven, Queen of hell,
Hornèd hunter of the night—
Lend your power unto the spell,
And work our will by magic rite!
By all the power of land and sea,
By all the might of moon and sun—
As we do will, so mote it be;
Chant the spell, and be it done!
Eko, Eko, Azarak,
Eko, Eko, Zomelak,   (repeated till ready)
Eko, Eko, Cernunnos,
Eko, Eko, Aradia!"

When the High Priestess decides it is time (and, if she has been weaving, has restored the coven to a plain ring), she orders:

"Down!"

The whole coven drops to the ground and sits in a ring facing inwards.

This is the end of the Opening Ritual. If the meeting were an Esbat, the High Priestess would now direct the particular work to be done. If it is a Sabbat, the appropriate ritual now begins.

One other short ritual should be set down here, to complete the picture: the Consecration of the Wine and Cakes. This takes place at every Esbat, usually after the work is over and before the coven relaxes within the Circle. At a Sabbat, both wine and cakes have to be consecrated if the Great Rite is actual (see Section II); if the Great Rite is symbolic, consecration of the wine is an integral part of it, leaving only the cakes to be consecrated by the usual ritual.

Consecration of the Wine and Cakes
A male witch kneels before a female witch in front of the altar. He holds up the chalice of wine to her; she holds her athame point downwards, and lowers the point into the wine. (See Plate 17.)
The man says:
"As the athame is to the male, so the cup is to the female; and conjoined, they become one in truth."

The woman lays down her athame on the altar and then kisses the man (who remains kneeling) and accepts the chalice from him. She sips the wine, kisses the man again and passes the chalice back to him. He sips, rises and gives it to another woman with a kiss.

The chalice is passed in this way around the whole coven, man-to-woman and woman-to-man (each time with a kiss) until everyone has sipped the wine.

If there is more work to be done, the chalice is now returned to the altar. If the coven is now ready to relax within the Circle, the chalice is placed between them as they sit on the floor, and anyone may drink from it as he or she wishes; the ritual passing-and-kissing is necessary only for the first time round. Nor, if the chalice is refilled during this relaxation, does it have to be re-consecrated.

To consecrate the cakes, the woman picks up her athame again, and the man, kneeling before her, holds up the dish of cakes. (See Plate 3.) She draws the Invoking Pentagram of Earth in the air above the cakes with her athame, while the man says:[15]

"O Queen most secret, bless this food into our bodies; bestowing health, wealth, strength, joy, and peace, and that fulfilment of love which is perfect happiness."

The woman lays down her athame on the altar, kisses the man and takes a cake from the dish. She kisses him again, and he takes a cake. He then rises and passes the dish to another woman with a kiss.

The dish is passed in this way round the whole coven, man-to-woman and woman-to-man (each time with a kiss), until everyone has taken a cake.

---

15 Adapted from Crowley's *Gnostic Mass.*

II The Great Rite

To say that the Great Rite is a ritual of male/female polarity is true but sounds a little coldly technical. To say that it is a sexual rite is also true but sounds (to the uninformed) like an orgy. In fact it is neither cold nor an orgy; so let us try to put it in proportion.

It can be enacted in either of two forms. It can be (and, we would guess, in most covens usually is) purely symbolic—in which case the whole coven is present the whole time. Or it can be 'actual'—that is to say, involving intercourse—in which case all of the coven except the man and woman concerned leave the Circle and the room, before the ritual becomes intimate, and do not return until they are summoned.

But whether it is symbolic or 'actual', witches make no apology for its sexual nature. To them, sex is holy—a manifestation of that essential polarity which pervades and activates the whole universe, from Macrocosm to Microcosm, and without which the universe would be inert and static—in other words, would not exist. The couple enacting the Great Rite are offering themselves, with reverence and joy, as expressions of the God and Goddess aspects of the Ultimate Source. "As above, so below." They are making themselves, to the best of their ability, channels for that divine polarity on *all* levels, from physical to spiritual. That is why it is called the *Great* Rite.

It is also why the 'actual' Great Rite is enacted without witnesses—not through shame but for the dignity of privacy. And it is why the Great Rite in its 'actual' form should, we feel, be enacted only by a married couple or by lovers of a marriage-like unity; because it *is* a magical rite, and a powerful one; and charged with the intensity of intercourse, by a couple whose relationship is less close, it may well activate links on levels for which they are unprepared and which may prove unbalanced and disturbing.

"Ritual sexual intercourse," says Doreen Valiente, "is a very old idea indeed—probably as old as humanity itself. Obviously, it is the very opposite of promiscuity. Intercourse for ritual purposes should be with a carefully selected partner, at the right time and in the right place. . . . It is love and only love that can give sex the spark of magic." (*Natural Magic* p. 110.)

The *symbolic* Great Rite, however, is a perfectly safe and beneficial ritual for two experienced witches at the level of friendship normal between members of the same coven. It is up to the High Priestess to decide who is suitable.

Perhaps a good way to express it would be to say that the 'actual' Great Rite is sex magic, while the symbolic Great Rite is the magic of gender.

The Great Rite invocation specifically declares that the body of the woman taking part is an altar, with her womb and generative organs as its sacred focus, and reveres it as such. It should hardly be necessary to emphasize to our readers that this has nothing to do with any 'Black Mass'—because the Black Mass itself had nothing to do with the Old Religion. The Black Mass was a *Christian* heresy, using perverted Christian forms, performed by sophisticated degenerates and unfrocked or corrupt priests, in which the living altar was used to desecrate the Christian Host. Such obscenity is of course utterly alien to the spirit and intent of the Great Rite.

In many sincere and honourable pagan religions, on the other hand, "there is one genuinely ancient figure—the naked woman upon the altar," Doreen Valiente points out, and goes on: "It would be more correct to say, the naked woman who is the altar; because this is her original role. . . . This use of a living woman's naked body as the altar where the forces of Life are worshipped and invoked goes back to before the beginnings of Christianity; back to the days of the ancient worship of the Great Goddess of Nature, in whom all things were one, under the image of Woman." (*An ABC of Witchcraft*, p. 44.)

In fact, not only the archetypal altar but every church, temple or synagogue *is* the body of the Goddess—psychologically, spiritually and in its historical evolution. The whole complex symbolism of ecclesiastical architecture bears this out beyond question, point by point; anyone who doubts it should read Lawrence Durdin-Robertson's richly documented (if confusingly presented) manual *The Symbolism of Temple Architecture*.

So Wiccan symbolism merely does vividly and naturally what other religions do obliquely and subconsciously.

At the Sabbats, the Great Rite is usually enacted by the High Priestess and High Priest. The Sabbats are special occasions, peaks of heightened awareness and significance in the witches' year; so it is fitting that at these festivals the coven leaders should take this key role upon themselves on the coven's behalf. However, rigid procedures are foreign to Wicca, and there may well be occasions when they decide that another couple should be named for the Sabbat Great Rite.

The Preparation

The only extra item needed for the Great Rite, whether symbolic or 'actual', is a veil at least a yard square. It should preferably be one of the Goddess colours—blue, green, silver or white.

The chalice should be filled with wine in readiness.

The High Priestess may also decide to change the music tape to something specially appropriate—possibly some music of personal significance to her and her partner. (For simplicity we are assuming, here and below, that it is the High Priestess and High Priest who are enacting the Rite.)

The Symbolic Ritual

If the cauldron is in the centre, it will be moved to the South of the Circle, unless the ritual indicates some other position.

The coven, except for the High Priestess and High Priest, arrange themselves around the perimeter of the Circle, man and woman alternately as far as possible, facing the centre.

The High Priestess and High Priest stand facing each other in the centre of the Circle, she with her back to the altar, he with his back to the South.

The High Priest gives the High Priestess the Fivefold Kiss.

The High Priestess then lays herself down face upwards, with her hips in the centre of the Circle, her head towards the altar, and her arms and legs outstretched to form the Pentagram.

The High Priest fetches the veil and spreads it over the High Priestess's body, covering her from breasts to knees. He then kneels facing her, with his knees between her feet. (See Plate 4.)

The High Priest calls a woman witch by name, to bring his athame from the altar. The woman witch does so and stands with the athame in her hands, a yard to the West of the High Priestess's hips and facing her.

The High Priest calls a man witch by name, to bring the chalice of wine from the altar. The man witch does so and stands with the chalice in his hands, a yard to the East of the High Priestess's hips and facing her.

The High Priest delivers the Invocation:

"Assist me to erect the ancient altar, at which in days past
     all worshipped;
The great altar of all things.
For in old time, Woman was the altar.
Thus was the altar made and placed,
And the sacred place was the point within the centre of the Circle.
As we have of old been taught that the point within the centre is
     the origin of all things,
Therefore should we adore it;
Therefore whom we adore we also invoke.
O Circle of Stars,
Whereof our father is but the younger brother,

Marvel beyond imagination, soul of infinite space,
Before whom time is ashamed, the mind bewildered, and the
    understanding dark,
Not unto thee may we attain unless thine image be love.
Therefore by seed and root, and stem and bud,
And leaf and flower and fruit do we invoke thee,
O Queen of Space, O Jewel of Light,
Continuous one of the heavens;
Let it be ever thus
That men speak not of thee as One, but as None;
And let them not speak of thee at all, since thou art continuous. [1]
For thou art the point within the Circle, which we adore;
The point of life, without which we would not be.
And in this way truly are erected the holy twin pillars; [2]
In beauty and in strength were they erected
To the wonder and glory of all men."

The High Priest removes the veil from the High Priestess's body, and hands it to the woman witch, from whom he takes his athame.

The High Priestess rises and kneels facing the High Priest, and takes the chalice from the man witch.

(Note that both these handings-over are done *without* the customary ritual kiss.)

The High Priest continues the Invocation:

    "Altar of mysteries manifold, [3]
    The sacred Circle's secret point—
    Thus do I sign thee as of old,
    With kisses of my lips anoint."

The High Priest kisses the High Priestess on the lips, and continues:

---

1. From *"O Circle of Stars"* down to *"since thou art continuous"*, this Book of Shadows invocation is taken from the *Gnostic Mass* in Aleister Crowley's *Magick.*
2. The "holy twin pillars" are Boaz and Jachin, which flanked the entrance to the Holy of Holies in Solomon's Temple. Boaz (coloured black) represents Severity ("strength"), and Jachin (white) Mildness ("beauty"). Cf. the Tree of Life and the High Priestess Tarot card. In the Great Rite, they are clearly symbolized by the woman-altar's legs.
3. From *"Altar of mysteries manifold"* to the end of the Invocation was written by Doreen Valiente, who also composed a fully rhyming version.

"Open for me the secret way,
The pathway of intelligence,
Beyond the gates of night and day,
Beyond the bounds of time and sense.
Behold the mystery aright—
The five true points of fellowship . . ."

The High Priestess holds up the chalice, and the High Priest lowers the point of his athame into the wine. (Both use both their hands for this—see Plate 19.) The High Priest continues:

"Here where the Lance and Grail unite,
And feet, and knees, and breast, and lip."

The High Priest hands his athame to the woman witch and then places both his hands round those of the High Priestess as she holds the chalice. He kisses her, and she sips the wine; she kisses him, and he sips the wine. Both of them keep their hands round the chalice while they do this.

The High Priest then takes the chalice from the High Priestess, and they both rise to their feet.

The High Priest hands the chalice to the woman witch with a kiss, and she sips; she passes the chalice to the man witch with a kiss, and he sips. From him, the chalice is passed man-to-woman, woman-to-man, round the coven, each time with a kiss, in the normal way.

The High Priestess and High Priest then consecrate the cakes, which are passed round in the normal way.

The 'Actual' Ritual

The 'actual' Great Rite follows the same procedure as the symbolic one above, with the following exceptions.

The woman and man witch are not summoned, and the athame and chalice remain on the altar.

When the High Priest reaches *"To the wonder and glory of all men"* in the Invocation, he stops. The Maiden then fetches her athame from the altar and ritually opens a gateway in the Circle by the door of the room. The coven file through and leave the room. The Maiden steps last out of the Circle, ritually seals the gateway behind her, lays her athame on the floor outside the Circle and leaves the room, closing the door behind her.

The High Priestess and High Priest are thus left alone in the room and the Circle.

The High Priest continues the Invocation to the end, but the actual details of enacting the Rite are now a private matter for him and the High Priestess. No member of the coven may question them on it afterwards, directly or indirectly.

When they are ready to re-admit the coven, the High Priest takes his athame from the altar, ritually opens the gateway, opens the door and summons the coven. He returns his athame to the altar.

The Maiden picks up her athame on the way in and ritually seals the gateway after the coven have re-entered the Circle. She returns her athame to the altar.

Wine and cakes are now consecrated in the normal way.

III   The Closing Ritual

A Magic Circle, once cast, must always and without exception be banished when the occasion or purpose for which it was cast is finished.[1] It would be bad manners not to thank, and bid farewell to, the entities you had invoked to guard it; bad magic to create a barrier on the astral plane and then to leave it undismantled, a stray obstacle like an upturned rake on a garden path; and bad psychology to have so little belief in its reality and effectiveness that you assume it will go away the moment you stop thinking about it.

---

1. The Rite of Hagiel, as described in Chapter XIV of *What Witches Do*, may appear to break this rule; but the special circumstances should be clear to careful readers of it. For one thing, the Lords of the Watchtowers are not summoned.

The Preparation

Strictly speaking, no preparation is needed for the ritual of banishing the Circle; but two provisions should be borne in mind, during your activities *in* the Circle, in anticipation of it.

First, if any objects have been consecrated in the Circle, they should be kept together—or at least each of them remembered—so that they can be picked up and carried by someone placed at the back of the coven during the banishing. To make the gestures of a Banishing Pentagram *towards* a newly consecrated object would have a neutralizing effect.

Second, you should see that at least one cake, or biscuit, and a little of the wine are left, so that these can be taken outside afterwards and scattered or poured as an offering to the Earth. (Living in Ireland, we follow local tradition by making this offering in a slightly different way; we leave it overnight in two little bowls, outside on a west-facing window-sill, for the *sidhe* (pronounced 'shee'), or fairy-folk. The *sidhe*, incidentally, are reputed to like a pat of butter on the cake or biscuit.)

The Ritual

The High Priestess faces the East with her athame in her hand. The High Priest stands to her right, and the rest of the coven stand behind them. All carry their athames, if they have them, except for the person carrying the newly-consecrated objects (if any) who stands right at the back. The Maiden (or someone detailed by the High Priestess for the purpose) stands near to the front, ready to blow out each candle in turn.

The High Priestess says:

"Ye Lords of the Watchtowers of the East, ye Lords of Air; we do thank you for attending our rites; and ere ye depart to your pleasant and lovely realms, we bid you hail and farewell. . . . Hail and farewell."

As she speaks, she draws the Banishing Pentagram of Earth with her athame in the air in front of her, thus:

Banishing

After drawing the Pentagram, she kisses her athame blade and lays it on her heart for a second or two.

The High Priest and the rest of the coven copy all these gestures with their own athames; any who are without athames use their right forefingers. (The bearer of the consecrated objects makes no gestures.) All say the second "*Hail and farewell*" with her.

The Maiden steps forward and blows out the East candle.

The whole procedure is repeated facing South, the High Priestess saying:

"*Ye Lords of the Watchtowers of the South, ye Lords of Fire; we do thank you . . .*" etc.

Then to the West, the High Priestess saying:

"*Ye Lords of the Watchtowers of the West, ye Lords of Water; ye Lords of Death and of Initiation; we do thank you . . .*" etc.

Then to the North, the High Priestess saying:

"*Ye Lords of the Watchtowers of the North, ye Lords of Earth; Boreas, thou guardian of the Northern portals; thou powerful God, thou gentle Goddess; we do thank you . . .*" etc.

At the North, the Maiden merely blows out the Earth candle; for purely practical reasons, she leaves the two altar candles burning until the room lights are turned on.

The Sabbat is over.

The Sabbats

IV   Imbolg, 2nd February

We have called the four Greater Sabbats by their Celtic names for consistency, and used the Irish Gaelic forms of those names for the reasons we gave on p. 14. But Imbolg is more commonly known, even among witches, by the pretty name of Candlemas under which it was Christianized—understandably enough, because this Feast of Lights can and should be a pretty occasion.

Imbolg is *i mbolg* (pronounced 'im*mol*'g', with a slight unstressed vowel between the 'l' and the 'g') which means 'in the belly'. It is the quickening of the year, the first foetal stirrings of Spring in the womb of Mother Earth. Like all the Celtic Great Sabbats, it is a fire festival—but here the emphasis is on light rather than heat, the strengthening spark of light beginning to pierce the gloom of Winter. (Farther south, where winter is less forbiddingly dark, the emphasis may be the other way; Armenian Christians, for example, light their new sacred fire of the year on Candlemas Eve, not Easter as elsewhere.)

The Moon is the light-symbol of the Goddess, and the Moon above all stands for her threefold aspect of Maid, Mother and Crone (Enchantment, Ripeness and Wisdom). Lunar light is particularly that of inspiration. So it is fitting that Imbolg should be the feast of Brigid (Brid, Brigante), the radiant triple Muse-Goddess, who is also a fertility-bringer; for at Imbolg, when the first trumpets of Spring can be heard in the distance, the spirit is quickened as well as the body and the Earth.

Brigid (who also gave her name to Brigantia, the Celtic kingdom of the whole of the North of England above a line from the Wash to Staffordshire) is a classic example of a pagan deity Christianized with little attempt to hide the fact—or as Frazer puts it in *The Golden Bough* (p. 177),[1] she is "an old heathen goddess of fertility, disguised in a threadbare Christian cloak". St Brigid's Day, *Lá Fhéile Bríd* (pronounced approximately 'law ella breed') in Ireland, is 1st February, the eve of Imbolg. The historical St Brigid lived from about AD 453–523; but her legends, characteristics and holy places are those of the Goddess Brid, and the folk-customs of St Brigid's Day in the Celtic lands are plainly pre-Christian. It is significant that Brigid is known as "the Mary of the Gael", for like Mary she transcends the human biographical data to fill man's "Goddess-shaped yearning" (see p. 139 below). Tradition, incidentally, says that St Brigid was brought up by a wizard and that she had the power to multiply food and drink to nourish the needy—including the delightful ability to turn her bath-water into beer.

The making of St Brigid's Crosses of rush or straw (and they are still widely made in Ireland, both at home and for the handicraft shops) "is probably derived from an ancient pre-Christian ceremony connected with the preparation of the seed

---

1. Every book reference in the text, with its publisher and date, and where necessary (as here, with *The Golden Bough*) the edition to which page references are made, is listed in the Bibliography at the end—together with some of the books we have found most useful in our study of seasonal traditions and mythology.

grain for growing in the Spring" (*The Irish Times*, 1st February 1977).

In Scotland, on the eve of St Brigid's Day, the women of the house would dress up a sheaf of oats in woman's clothing and lay it in a basket called 'Brigid's bed', side by side with a phallic club. They would then call out three times: "Brid is come, Brid is welcome!" and leave candles burning by the 'bed' all night. If the impression of the club was found in the ashes of the hearth in the morning, the year would be fruitful and prosperous. The ancient meaning is clear: with the use of appropriate symbols, the women of the house prepare a place for the Goddess and make her welcome, and invite the fertilizing God to come and impregnate her. Then they discreetly withdraw—and, when the night is over, return to look for a sign of the God's visit (his footprint by the fire of the Goddess of Light?). If the sign is there, their invocation has succeeded, and the year is pregnant with the hoped-for bounty.

In the Isle of Man, a similar ritual was carried out; there, the occasion was called *Laa'l Breeshey*. In Northern England—the old Brigantia, Candlemas was known as 'the Wives' Feast Day'.

The welcoming ritual is still part of *Lá Fhéile Bríd* in many Irish homes. Philomena Rooney of Wexford, whose family live near the Leitrim-Donegal border, tells us she still goes home for it whenever she can. While her grandparents were still alive, the whole family would gather at their house on St Brigid's Eve, 31st January. Her uncle would have gathered a cartload of rushes from the farm and would bring them to the door at midnight. The ritual is always the same.

"The person bringing the rushes to the house covers his or her head and knocks on the door. The *Bean an Tighe* (woman of the house) sends someone to open the door and says to the person entering "*Fáilte leat a Bhríd*" ("Welcome, Brigid"), to which the person entering replies "*Beannacht Dé ar daoine an tighe seo*" ("God bless the people of this house"). The holy water is sprinkled on the rushes, and everyone joins in making the crosses. When the crosses are made, the remaining rushes are buried, following which everyone joins in a meal. On 1st February last year's crosses are burned and replaced with the newly made ones."

In Philomena's family, two types were made. Her grandmother, who came from North Leitrim, made the Celtic Cross, equal-armed and enclosed in a circle. Her grandfather, who came from South Donegal, made the plain equal-armed cross. She supposes that these were local traditional styles.[2] Great importance was attached to the burning of last year's crosses. "We have this thing that you should never throw it out, you should burn it." Here again is the theme which recurs throughout the year's ritual cycle: the magical importance of fire.

In Ireland, this land of magic wells (over three thousand Irish holy wells are listed), there are probably more wells of Brigid than there are even of St Patrick—which is hardly surprising, because the lady was here first by untold centuries. There is a *tobar Bhríd* (Brigid's Well) barely a mile from our first Irish home, near Ferns in County Wexford, in a neighbouring farmer's field; it is a very ancient spring, and the locality is known to have been holy to Brigid for a good thousand years, and doubtless for a very long time before that. The farmer (regretfully, for he is sensitive to tradition) had to cover the well with a rock because it had become a danger to children. But he told us there were always bits of cloth[3] to be seen tied to nearby

---

2. Local patterns of the Brigid's Crosses do vary considerably. Philomena's 'plain' cross in fact has the four arms woven in separately with their roots off-centre, producing a swastika (fire-wheel) effect. This is also our County Mayo type, though we have also seen single and multiple diamond patterns. A County Armagh type given to us by a friend has each of the two crosspieces consisting of three bundles, interlacing with the other three at the centre, and we have seen similar ones from Counties Galway, Clare and Kerry; memory perhaps of 'the Three Brigids', the original Triple Muse Goddess? (See *The White Goddess*, pp. 101, 394 and elsewhere.) A County Derry example has five bands instead of three, and a West Donegal one has a triple vertical and a single horizontal. Such local diversity shows how deep-rooted the folk custom is. The Brigid's Cross in the fire-wheel form, with three-banded arms, is the symbol of Radio Telefís Éireann.
3. These pieces of cloth probably symbolize clothing. Gypsy women, in their famous annual pilgrimage to Saintes-Maries-de-la-Mer in southern France on 24th and 25th May, leave items of clothing, representing the absent or sick, in the crypt-shrine of their patroness Black Sara. "The ceremonial is clearly not original. The rite of hanging up garments is known among the Dravidians of northern India who 'believe in fact that the linen and clothes of a sick person become impregnated with his malady, and that the patient will be cured if his linen is purified by contact with a sacred tree'. Hence, among them are seen trees or images covered with rags of clothing which they call *Chitraiya*

bushes, put there secretly by people invoking Brid's help as they had done since time immemorial; and we could, literally, still feel the power of the place by laying our hands on the rock.

(Incidentally, if like most witches you believe in the magic of names, you should pronounce Brid or Bride as 'Breed' and *not* to rhyme with 'hide' as it has been somewhat harshly anglicized—for example in London's own *tobar Bhríd*, Bridewell.)

In ancient Rome, February was cleansing time—*Februarius mensis*, 'the month of ritual purification'. At its beginning came the Lupercalia, when the Luperci, the priests of Pan, ran through the streets naked except for a goatskin girdle and carrying goatskin thongs. With these they struck everybody who passed, and in particular married women, who were believed to be made fertile thereby. This ritual was both popular and patrician (Mark Antony is on record as having performed the Lupercus role) and survived for centuries into the Christian era. Women developed the habit of stripping themselves as well, to allow the Luperci more scope. Pope Gelasius I, who reigned AD 492–6, banned this cheerfully scandalous festival and met with such an outcry that he had to apologize. It was finally abolished at the beginning of the next century.

Lupercalia aside, the tradition of February cleansing remained strong. Doreen Valiente says in *An ABC of Witchcraft Past and Present*: "The evergreens for Yuletide decorations were holly, ivy, mistletoe, the sweet-smelling bay and rosemary, and green branches of the box tree. By Candlemas, all had to be gathered up and burnt, or hobgoblins would haunt the house. In other words, by that time a new tide of life had

---

Bhavani, 'Our Lady of the Rags'. There exists likewise a 'Tree for Tatters' (*sinderich ogateh*) among the Kirghiz of the Sea of Aral. One could probably find other examples of this magical prophylaxis." (Jean-Paul Clébert, *The Gypsies*, p. 143.) One can indeed. We wonder, for example, why Irish itinerants always seem to leave some clothing behind on the bushes by an abandoned camp-site. They are notoriously untidy, it is true, but many of these garments are by no means rubbish. One magic well near Wexford town was consecrated to no saint or deity, yet was much venerated; its cloth-laden bush, local historian Nicky Furlong records, "was chopped down by a normally well-adjusted clergyman. That ended the secret cult. (He died very suddenly afterwards, God rest him.)"

started to flow through the whole world of nature, and people had to get rid of the past and look to the future. Spring-cleaning was originally a nature ritual." In some parts of Ireland, we find, there is a tradition of leaving the Christmas tree in place (stripped of its decorations but retaining its lights) until Candlemass; if it has kept its green needles, good luck and fruitfulness are assured for the year ahead.

One other strange Candlemas belief is widespread in the British Isles, France, Germany and Spain: that fine weather on Candlemas Day means more Winter to come, but bad weather on that day means that Winter is over. Perhaps this is a kind of 'touch wood' acknowledgement of the fact that Candlemas is the natural turning-point between Winter and Spring, and so to be impatient about it is unlucky.

In the Candlemas ritual in the Book of Shadows, the High Priestess invokes the God into the High Priest, instead of him invoking the Goddess into her. Perhaps this too, like the Scottish 'Brigid's bed' tradition, is really a seasonal invitation to the God to impregnate the Earth Mother. We have kept to this procedure and retained the form of the invocation.

The Book of Shadows also mentions the (sixteenth-century) Volta Dance; but we wonder if what is really meant is the very much older traditional witches' dance in which the man and woman link arms back-to-back. We have therefore used this earlier dance.

In Christian tradition, the Crown of Lights is often worn by a very young girl, presumably to symbolize the extreme youth of the year. This is perfectly valid, of course; but we, with our Triple Goddess enactment, prefer to allot it to the Mother—because it is Mother Earth who is quickened at Imbolg.

The Preparation

The High Priestess selects two woman witches who, with herself, will represent the Triple Goddess—Maid (Enchantment), Mother (Ripeness) and Crone (Wisdom)—and allocates the three roles.

A Crown of Lights is prepared for the Mother and left on or by the altar. Traditionally, the Crown should be of candles or tapers, which are lit during the ritual; but this requires care, and some people may be wary of it. If a candle or taper Crown is made, it should be constructed firmly enough to hold them without wobbling and should incorporate a cap to protect the hair against dripping wax. (You can work wonders with kitchen foil.)

We have found that birthday-cake candles, which can be bought in packets almost anywhere, make an ideal Crown of Lights. They weigh practically nothing, hardly drip at all and burn quite long enough for the purpose of the ritual. A very simple birthday-candle crown can be made as follows. Get a roll of self-adhesive tape about three-quarters of an inch wide (the plain-coloured plastic kind is suitable) and cut off a length four or five inches longer than the circumference of the lady's head. Pin this, sticky side *upwards*, to a board. Stick the bottom ends of the candles across this, spaced about one and half inches apart, but leaving a good three inches of each end of the tape empty. Now cut a second piece of the tape of the same length as the first, hold it sticky side *downwards*, and apply it carefully to the first tape, moulding it around the base of each candle. Unpin the ends, and you now have a neat band of candles which can be wrapped round the head, the free ends being secured together by a safety-pin at the back. The candle-band should be wrapped around a kitchen-foil skull-cap which has been moulded to the head beforehand; the foil can then be trimmed to match the bottom edge of the band. You can see the finished result in use in Plate 5; in that case, it has been improved still further by fitting foil and candle-band inside an existing copper crown.

(Incidentally, that copper crown—seen closer in Plate 10— with its crescent-moon front was made for Janet by our coppersmith friend Peter Clark of Tintine, The Rower, County Kilkenny. Peter supplies beautiful ritual equipment in copper or bronze, either from stock or made to your own require-ments.)

An alternative form of the Crown of Lights, avoiding the wax-dripping risk, is a handyman's job—a crown incorporating a number of flashlamp bulbs, soldered to their leads, with small batteries concealed under a Foreign-Legion-type piece of fabric falling over the neck; the 'switch' being a small crocodile-clip, or simply two bared wire-ends can be twisted together. This bulb-crown can be kept from year to year, and decorated with fresh foliage each time. (It does, however, require some experiment in the construction, both as to the distribution of the weight of the batteries and as to the components and wiring; too many bulbs in parallel will give a fine light for the first minute and then fade rapidly because of the excessive drain.) If you do not like either of these, the third possibility is a crown incorporating little mirrors—as many as possible of them, facing outwards to catch the light.

A bundle of straw a foot to eighteen inches long, with a straw crosspiece for arms, should be dressed in woman's clothing—a doll's dress will do, or simply a cloth pinned round. If you possess a corn dolly of suitable shape for dressing (a Brigid's Cross is ideal), this may be even better. (See Plate 6.) This figure is called a 'Biddy'—or, if you prefer the Gaelic, '*Brídeóg*' (pronounced 'breed-oge').

You also need a phallic wand, which can be a simple staff about the same length as the Biddy; though, since the Book of Shadows rituals frequently call for a phallic wand as distinct from the coven's 'normal' one, it is worth while making yourselves a permanent version. Ours is a piece of thin branch with a pine-cone secured to the tip, and black and white ribbons spiralling in opposite directions along the shaft. (See Plate 6).

Biddy and wand should be ready beside the altar, together with two unlit candles in candle-holders.

Also beside the altar is a small bouquet of greenery (as springlike as possible and incorporating spring flowers if you can get them) for the woman who portrays the Maid; and a dark-coloured scarf or cloak for the Crone.

The broomstick (the traditional witch's besom of twigs) is by the altar too.

The cauldron, with a candle burning inside it, is placed beside the South candle. By the cauldron are laid three or four twigs of evergreen or dried vegetation such as holly, ivy, mistletoe, bay, rosemary or box.

If, like us, you follow the tradition of keeping the Christmas Tree (without its decorations but with its lights) in the house till Candlemas, it should, if practicable, be in the room where the Circle is held, with all its lights lit.

The Ritual

The Opening Ritual is shorter for Imbolg. The High Priest does not Draw Down the Moon on the High Priestess, nor does he make the *"Great God Cernunnos"* invocation; and the Charge is not declaimed until later.

After the Witches' Rune, all the working partners (including the High Priestess and High Priest) dance back-to-back in couples, with their arms hooked through each other's elbows. Unpartnered witches dance solo, though after a while partners break up and re-combine with unpartnered ones, so that everybody can take part.

When the High Priestess decides that the dancing has gone on long enough, she stops it, and the coven arrange themselves around the Circle facing inwards. The High Priest stands with his back to the altar, and the High Priestess faces him.

The High Priest gives the High Priestess the Fivefold Kiss; then she in turn gives him the Fivefold Kiss. The High Priest takes the wand in his right hand and the scourge in his left, and assumes the Osiris Position (see p. 40).

The High Priestess, facing the High Priest as he stands before the altar, invokes:[4]

> *"Dread Lord of Death and Resurrection,*
> *Of Life, and the Giver of Life;*
> *Lord within ourselves, whose name is Mystery of Mysteries,*
> *Encourage our hearts,*
> *Let thy Light crystallize itself in our blood,*
> *Fulfilling of us resurrection;*
> *For there is no part of us that is not of the Gods.*
> *Descend, we pray thee, upon thy servant and priest."*

The High Priest draws the Invoking Pentagram of Earth in the air, towards the High Priestess, and says:

"Blessed be."

The High Priest steps to one side, while the High Priestess and the women of the coven prepare 'Brigid's bed'. They lay the Biddy and the phallic wand side by side in the centre of the Circle, with the heads towards the altar. They place the

---

4. Lines 3–5 of this invocation are from Crowley's *Gnostic Mass.*

candlesticks on either side of the 'bed' and light the candles. (See Plate 6.)

High Priestess and women stand around the 'bed' and say together:

"*Brid is come—Brid is welcome!*" (Repeated three times.)

The High Priest lays down his wand and scourge on the altar. The High Priestess summons the two selected women; she and they now assume their Triple Goddess roles. (See Plate 5.) The Mother stands with her back to the centre of the altar, and the High Priest crowns her with the Crown of Lights; the Maid and Crone arrange her hair becomingly, and the High Priest lights the tapers on the Crown (or switches on the bulbs).

The Crone now stands beside the Mother, to her left, and the High Priest and Maid drape the shawl or cloak over her shoulders.

The Maid now stands beside the Mother, to her right, and the High Priest puts the bouquet into her hands.

The High Priest goes to the South, where he stands facing the three women. He declaims:

> "*Behold the Three-Formed Goddess;*
> *She who is ever Three—Maid, Mother and Crone;*
> *Yet is she ever One.*
> *For without Spring there can be no Summer,*
> *Without Summer, no Winter,*
> *Without Winter, no new Spring.*"

The High Priest then delivers the Charge in its entirety, from "*Listen to the words of the Great Mother*" right to "*that which is attained at the end of desire*"—but substituting "she, her, hers" for "I, me, my, mine".

When he has finished, the Maid takes up the broomstick and makes her way slowly deosil round the Circle, ritually sweeping it clear of all that is old and outworn. The Mother and the Crone walk behind her in stately procession. The Maid then replaces the broom beside the altar, and the three women resume their places in front of the altar.

The High Priest then turns and kneels before the cauldron. He picks up each of the evergreen twigs in turn, sets fire to each from the cauldron candle, blows the twig out and puts it in the cauldron beside the candle. (This symbolic burning is all that is advisable in a small room, because of smoke; out of doors, or in a large room, they may be burned away completely.)

As he does this, he declaims:

> *"Thus we banish winter,*
> *Thus we welcome spring;*
> *Say farewell to what is dead,*
> *And greet each living thing.*
> *Thus we banish winter,*
> *Thus we welcome spring!"*

The High Priest goes to the Mother, blows out or switches off the Crown of Lights and removes it from the Mother's head. On this signal, the Maid lays her bouquet, and the Crone her shawl or cloak, beside the altar, and the High Priest lays the Crown of Lights there also.

The High Priest steps aside, and the three women fetch the Biddy, the phallic wand and the candles (which they extinguish) from the centre of the Circle and lay them beside the altar.

The Great Rite is now enacted.

After the Cakes and Wine, a suitable game for Imbolg is the Candle Game. The men sit in a ring facing inwards, close enough to reach each other, and the women stand behind them. The men pass a lighted candle deosil from hand to hand, while the women (without stepping inside the ring of men) lean forward and try to blow it out. When a woman succeeds, she gives three flicks of the scourge to the man who was holding it at the time, and he gives her the Fivefold Kiss in return. The candle is then relit and the game continues.

If the custom of keeping the Christmas Tree till Candlemas has been observed, the Tree must be taken out of the house and disposed of as soon as possible after the ritual.

V   Spring Equinox, 21st March

"The Sun," as Robert Graves puts it, "arms himself at the Spring Equinox." Light and dark are in balance, but the light is mastering the darkness. It is basically a solar festival, and a newcomer to the Old Religion in Celtic and Teutonic Europe. Although Teutonic influence—Margaret Murray's "solstitial invaders"—added Yule and Midsummer to the four Great Sabbats of the pastoral Celts, the new synthesis still embraced only six Festivals. "The Equinoxes," says Murray, "were never observed in Britain" (except, as we now know, by the pre-Celtic Megalithic peoples—see p. 14).

Yet the Equinoxes are now unquestionably with us; modern pagans, almost universally, celebrate the eight Festivals, and no one suggests that the two Equinoxes are an innovation thought up by Gerald Gardner or by Druid Revival romantics. They are a genuine part of pagan tradition as it exists today, even if their seeds blew in from the Mediterranean and germinated in the soil of the underground centuries, along with many other fruitful elements. (Wiccan purists who reject anything that stems from classical Greece or Rome, from Ancient Egypt, from the Hebrew Qabala or from the Tuscan *Aradia*, had better stop celebrating the Equinoxes, too.) The importing of such concepts is always a complex process. Folk-awareness of the Spring Equinox in the British Isles, for example, must have been mainly imported with the Christian Easter. But Easter brought in its luggage, so to speak, the Mediterranean pagan overtones of the Spring Equinox.

The difficulty which faces witches in deciding just how to celebrate the Spring Equinox Sabbat is not that the 'foreign' associations are in fact alien to the native ones but that they overlap with them, expressing themes that had long ago become attached to the older native Sabbats. For instance, the sacrificial mating theme in Mediterranean lands has strong links with the Spring Equinox. The grim festival of the Phrygian goddess Cybele, at which the self-castration, death and resurrection of her son/lover Attis was marked by worshippers castrating themselves to become her priests, was from 22nd to 25th March. In Rome these rites took place on the spot where St Peter's now stands in Vatican City. In fact, in places where Attis-worship was widespread, the local Christians used to celebrate the death and resurrection of Christ at the same date; and pagans and Christians used to quarrel bitterly about which of their gods was the true prototype and which the imitation. On sheer chronology, there should have been no dispute, because Attis came from Phrygia many centuries before Christ; but the Christians had the unanswerable argument that the Devil cunningly placed counterfeits ahead of the true Coming in order to deceive mankind.

Easter—Jesus's willing death, descent into Hell and resurrection—can be seen as the Christian version of the sacrificial mating theme, for 'Hell' in this sense is patriarchal monotheism's **view** of the collective unconscious, the dreaded feminine **aspect**, the Goddess, into whom the sacrificed God is plunged as the necessary prelude to rebirth. Christ's 'Harrowing of Hell', as described in the apocryphal Gospel of

Nicodemus, involved his rescuing of the souls of the just from Adam onwards "who had fallen asleep since the beginning of the world" and his raising of them to Heaven. Stripped of theological dogma, this can have a positive meaning—the re-integration of the buried treasures of the unconscious ('the gift of the Goddess') with the light of analytical consciousness ('the gift of the God').

Spring, too, was a particular season in classical and pre-classical times for a form of the sacrificial mating which was also kindlier and more positive than the Attis cult—the *Hieros gamos*, or sacred marriage. In this, woman identified herself with the Goddess, and man sank himself into the Goddess through her, giving of his masculinity but not destroying it, and emerging from the experience spiritually revitalized. The Great Rite, whether symbolic or actual, is obviously the witches' *hieros gamos*; and then, as now, it shocked many people who did not understand it.[1] (For a profound Jungian commentary on the *hieros gamos*, see M. Esther Harding's *Woman's Mysteries*.)

But in the North, where Spring comes later, these aspects really belonged to Bealtaine instead of to the unobserved

---

1. The most savage opponents of the *hieros gamos* and all it stood for were of course the Hebrew prophets. Their tirades against "harlotry" and "whoring after strange gods", with which the Old Testament abounds, were political, not ethical. The Goddess-worship which surrounded them, and to which ordinary Hebrew families still clung for centuries alongside the official Yahweh-worship, was a direct threat to the patriarchal system they were trying to enforce. For unless every woman was an exclusive chattel of her husband, and a virgin on marriage, how could paternity be certain? And unquestionable paternity was the keystone of the whole system. Hence the Biblical death-penalty for adulteresses, for brides found to be non-virgin and even for the victims of rape (unless they were neither married nor betrothed, in which case they had to marry the rapist); the ruthlessness with which the Hebrews, "according to the word of the Lord", massacred the entire population of conquered Canaanite cities, men, women and children (except for any attractive virgins, whom "the word of the Lord" permitted them to kidnap as wives); and even the Levitic rewriting of the Creation myth to give divine sanction to male superiority (it is interesting that the Serpent and the Tree were both universally recognized Goddess-symbols). From this ancient political battle, Christianity (outdoing even Judaism and Islam) inherited the hatred of sex, the warped asceticism and the contempt for women that has bedevilled it from St Paul onwards and is still far from dead. (See again Merlin Stone's *Paradise Papers*.)

Equinox; and it is at Bealtaine, as will be seen, that we have placed our corresponding 'Love Chase' ritual. It is perhaps significant that Easter (owing to the complex lunar method of dating it) reflects this overlap by falling anywhere from just after the Equinox to just before Bealtaine. Easter, by the way, is named after the Teutonic goddess Eostre, whose name is probably yet another variant of Ishtar, Astarte and Aset (the correct Egyptian name 'Isis' being the Greek form). Eostre's spring rites bore a family resemblance to those of the Babylonian Ishtar. Another piece of pagan 'luggage'!

But if in the human-fertility aspect the Spring Equinox must bow to Bealtaine, it can properly retain the vegetation-fertility aspect, even if in the North it marks a different stage of it. Round the Mediterranean, the Equinox is the time of sprouting; in the North, it is the time of sowing. As a solar festival, too, it must share with the Greater Sabbats the eternal theme of fire and light, which has survived strongly in Easter folklore. In many parts of Europe, particularly Germany, Easter bonfires are lit with fire obtained from the priest, on traditional hilltop sites often known locally as 'Easter Mountain''. (Relic of earlier, larger-scale customs—see under Bealtaine, p. 82) As far as the light shines, it is believed, the land will be fruitful and the homes secure. And, as always, people jump the dying embers, and cattle are driven over them.

The Book of Shadows says that for this festival, "the symbol of the Wheel should be placed on the Altar, flanked with burning candles, or fire in some form." So, assuming this to be one of the genuine traditional elements which Gardner was given, we can take it that British witches, in absorbing the 'non-native' Equinoxes into their calendar, used the fire-wheel symbol which also features in many midsummer folk-customs throughout Europe.

A hint that the solar fire-wheel *is* a genuine equinoctial tradition, and not merely a gap-filling choice of Gardner's, may be found in the custom of wearing shamrock on St Patrick's Day—which falls on 17th March. According to the usual explanation, the shamrock became Ireland's national emblem because St Patrick once used its three-leaved shape to illustrate the doctrine of the Trinity. But the *Oxford English Dictionary* says this tradition is 'late'; and in fact the first printed reference to it was in an eighteenth-century botanical work. And Dinneen's *Irish-English Dictionary*, defining *seamróg*, says its use as a national emblem in Ireland (and, incidentally, in Hanover, in the home territory of the "solstitial invaders") is possibly "a survival of the trignetra, a Christianized wheel or sun symbol", and adds that the four-leaved variety is "believed to bring luck, related to an early apotropaic sign enclosed in a circle (sun or wheel symbol)".

The St Patrick's Day shamrock has become standardized as the lesser yellow trefoil (*Trifolium dubius* or *minus*), but in Shakespeare's day 'shamrock' meant wood sorrel, *Oxalis acetosella*; and Dinneen defines *seamróg* as "a shamrock, trefoil, clover, a bunch of green grass". Culpeper's *Complete Herbal* says "all the Sorrels are under the dominion of Venus." So the threefold spring-green leaves in the Irishman's equinox buttonhole bring us back not only to the Sun God but also, through the modern screen of the Trinity, to the Triple Goddess. (Artemis, the Greek Triple Moon Goddess, fed her hinds on trefoil.)

And as for the lucky four-leaved variety—any Jungian psychologist (and the Lords of the Watchtowers!) will tell you that the quartered circle is an archetypal symbol of wholeness and balance. The solar fire-wheel, the Celtic cross, the four-leaved shamrock, the Magic Circle with its four cardinal candles, the Egyptian hieroglyph *niewt* meaning 'town', the Easter hot-cross bun, the Byzantine basilica—all deliver the same immemorial message, much older than Christianity.

The Easter egg, too, is pre-Christian. It is the World Egg, laid by the Goddess and split open by the heat of the Sun God; "and the hatching-out of the world was celebrated each year at the Spring festival of the Sun" (Graves, *The White Goddess*, pp. 248–9). Originally it was a snake's egg; the caduceus of Hermes portrays the coupling snakes, Goddess and God, who produced it. But under the influence of the Orphic mysteries, as Graves points out, "since the cock was the Orphic bird of resurrection, sacred to Apollo's son Aesculapius the healer, hens' eggs took the place of snakes' in the later Druidic mysteries and were coloured scarlet in the Sun's honour; and became Easter eggs." (Decorated eggs boiled in an infusion of furze blossom were rolled down hillsides in Ireland on Easter Monday.)

Stewart wrote in *What Witches Do*: "The Spring Equinox is obviously an occasion for decorating the room with daffodils and other spring blossoms, and also for honouring one of the younger women by appointing her the coven's Spring Queen and sending her home afterwards with an armful of the flowers." We have kept to this pleasant little custom.

The Preparation

A wheel symbol stands on the altar; it may be anything that feels suitable—a cut-out disc painted yellow or gold and decorated with spring flowers, a circular mirror, a round brass tray; ours is a 14-inch drumkit cymbal, highly polished and with a daffodil or primrose posy in its central hole.

The High Priest's robe (if any) and accessories should be symbolic of the Sun; any metal he wears should be gold, gilt, brass or bronze.

The altar and room should be decorated with spring flowers—particularly the yellow ones such as daffodils, primroses, gorse or forsythia. One bouquet should be ready for handing to the Spring Queen, and a chaplet of flowers for her crowning.

The cauldron is placed in the centre of the Circle, with an unlit candle inside it. A taper is ready on the altar for the Maiden to carry fire to the High Priest.

A phallic wand is ready on the altar.

Half as many cords as there are people present are ready on the altar, tied together at their centre-point in a single knot. (If there is an odd number of people, add one before dividing by two; e.g., for nine people take five cords.)

If you like, you can have a bowl of hard-boiled eggs, with painted shells (scarlet all over, or decorated as you wish), on the altar—one for each person plus one for the *sidhe* or earth-offering. These can be handed out during the feasting.

The Ritual

The Opening Ritual proceeds as usual, but without the Witches' Rune.

The High Priest stand in the East, and the High Priestess in the West, facing each other across the cauldron. The High Priestess carries the phallic wand in her right hand. The rest of the coven distribute themselves around the perimeter of the Circle.

The High Priestess says:[2]

> *"We kindle this fire today*
> *In presence of the Holy Ones,*
> *Without malice, without jealousy, without envy,*
> *Without fear of aught beneath the Sun*
> *But the High Gods.*
> *Thee we invoke, O Light of Life,*
> *Be Thou a bright flame before us,*
> *Be Thou a guiding star above us,*
> *Be Thou a smooth path beneath us;*
> *Kindle Thou within our hearts*
> *A flame of love for our neighbours,*
> *To our foes, to our friends, to our kindred all,*
> *To all men on the broad earth.*
> *O merciful Son of Cerridwen,*
> *From the lowliest thing that liveth*
> *To the Name which is highest of all."*

The High Priestess holds the phallic wand on high and walks slowly deosil round the cauldron to stand in front of the High Priest. She says:

"O Sun, be Thou armed to conquer the Dark!"

The High Priestess presents the phallic wand to the High Priest and then steps to one side.

The High Priest holds up the phallic wand in salute and replaces it on the altar.

The Maiden lights the taper from one of the altar candles and

---

2. Adapted by Doreen Valiente from two Scottish Gaelic blessings in Alexander Carmichael's *Carmina Gadelica* (see Bibliography). Carmichael, who lived 1832–1912, collected and translated a rich harvest of Gaelic prayers and blessings, handed down by word of mouth in the Highlands and Islands of Scotland. As Doreen says, "This beautiful old poetry is really sheer paganism with a thin Christian veneer." The six-volume *Carmina Gadelica*, though a treasure to own, is expensive; fortunately a selection of the English translations has been published as a recent paperback *The Sun Dances* (see Bibliography). The two sources Doreen used here will be found on pages 231 and 49 of volume I of *Carmina Gadelica*, and on pages 3 and 11 of *The Sun Dances*; Carmichael obtained them from crofters' wives in North Uist and Lochaber, respectively.

presents it to the High Priest. The Maiden then steps to one side.

The High Priest carries the taper to the cauldron and lights the cauldron candle with it. He gives the taper back to the Maiden, who blows it out and replaces it on the altar, picking up the cords instead.

The Maiden gives the cords to the High Priest.

The High Priestess arranges everybody round the cauldron, man facing woman as far as possible. The High Priest hands out the ends of the cords in accordance with her instructions, retaining one end of the final cord himself and handing the other end of it to the High Priestess. (If there is an odd number of people, with more women than men, he retains two cord-ends himself or, with more men than women, hands two cord-ends to the High Priestess; in either case, he must be linked with two women or she with two men.)

When everyone is holding a cord, they all pull the cords taut, with the central knot above the cauldron. They then start circling deosil in the Wheel Dance, to the Witches' Rune, building up speed, always keeping the cords taut and the knot over the cauldron.

The Wheel Dance continues till the High Priestess cries "*Down!*", and the coven all sit in a circle round the cauldron. The High Priest gathers up the cords (being careful not to let them drop on to the candle-flame) and replaces them on the altar.

The cauldron is then moved to beside the East candle, and the Great Rite is enacted.

After the Great Rite, the High Priest names a woman witch as the Spring Queen and stands her in front of the altar. He crowns her with the chaplet of flowers and gives her the Fivefold Kiss.

The High Priest then calls forward each man in turn to give the Spring Queen the Fivefold Kiss. When the last man has done so, the High Priest presents the Spring Queen with her bouquet.

The cauldron is replaced in the centre of the Circle, and, starting with the Spring Queen, everyone jumps the cauldron, singly or in couples—not forgetting to wish.

The cauldron-jumping over, the party begins.

VI   Bealtaine, 30th April

In the Celtic tradition, the two greatest festivals of all are
Bealtaine and Samhain—the beginning of Summer and the
beginning of Winter. To the Celts, as to all pastoral peoples, the
year had two seasons, not four; subtler divisions concerned
crop-raisers rather than cattle-raisers. Beltane, the anglicized
form, corresponds to the modern Irish Gaelic word *Bealtaine*
(pronounced 'b'*yol*-tinnuh', approximately rhyming with
'winner'), the name of the month of May, and to the Scottish
Gaelic word *Bealtuinn* (pronounced 'b'*yal*-ten', with the 'n' like
'ni' in 'onion'), meaning May Day.

The original meaning is 'Bel-fire'—the fire of the Celtic or
proto-Celtic god variously known as Bel, Beli, Balar, Balor or
the latinized Belenus—names traceable back to the Middle
Eastern Baal, which simply means 'Lord'.[1] Some people have

suggested that Bel is the British-Celtic equivalent of the Gaulish-Celtic Cernunnos; that may be true in the sense that both are archetypal male-principle deities, mates of the Great Mother, but we feel that the evidence points to their being different aspects of that principle. Cernunnos is always represented as the Horned God; he is above all a nature deity, the god of animals, the Celtic Pan. (Herne the Hunter, who haunts Windsor Great Park with his Wild Hunt, is a later English Cernunnos, as his name suggests.) He is also sometimes seen as a chthonic (underworld) deity, the Celtic Pluto. Originally, the Horned God was doubtless the tribal totem animal, whose mating with the Great Mother would have been the key fertility ritual of the totemic period. (See Lethbridge's *Witches; Investigating an Ancient Religion*, pp. 25–27.)

Bel, on the other hand, was 'the Bright One', god of light and fire. He had Sun-like qualities (classical writers equated him with Apollo) but he was not, strictly speaking, a Sun-God; as we have pointed out, the Celts were not solar-oriented. No people who worshipped the Sun as a god would give it a feminine name—and *grian* (Irish and Scottish Gaelic for 'Sun') is a feminine noun. So is *Mór*, a personalized Irish name for the Sun, as in the greeting '*Mór dhuit*'—'May the Sun bless you.' It may seem a subtle difference, but a god-symbol is not always regarded as *the same thing* as the god himself by his worshippers. Christians do not worship a lamb or a dove, nor did ancient Egyptians worship a baboon or a hawk; yet the first two are symbols of Christ and the Holy Spirit, and the second two of Thoth and Horus. To some people the Sun *was* a god, but not to the Celts with their feminine Sun, even though Bel/Balor, Oghma, Lugh and Llew had solar *attributes*. A traditional Scottish Gaelic folk-prayer (see Kenneth Jackson's *Celtic Miscellany*, item 34) addresses the Sun as "happy mother of the stars", rising "like a young queen in flower". (For further evidence that the pagan Celts' ritual calendar was oriented to the natural vegetation year and herd-raising, and not to the solar year and agriculture, see Frazer's *Golden Bough*, pp. 828–830.)

---

1. Of family interest to us: Janet's maiden name was Owen, and Owen family tradition claims descent from the Canaanite lords of Shechem, who themselves claimed to be of the seed of Baal.

Symbolically, both the Cernunnos aspect and the Bel aspect can be seen as ways of visualizing the Great Father who impregnates the Great Mother.[2] And these are the two themes which dominate the May Eve/May Day festival throughout Celtic and British folklore: fertility and fire.

The Bel-fires were lit on the hilltops to celebrate the return of life and fertility to the world. In the Scottish Highlands as late as the eighteenth century, Robert Graves tells us (*The White Goddess*, p. 416), fire was kindled by drilling an oak-plank, "but only in the kindling of the Beltane need-fire, to which miraculous virtue was ascribed. . . . It originally culminated in the sacrifice of a man representing the Oak-god." (It is interesting that in Rome the Vestal Virgins, guardians of the sacred fire, used to throw manikins made of rushes into the River Tiber at the May full moon as symbolic human sacrifices.)

In pagan Ireland no one could light a Bealtaine fire until the Ard Ri, the High King, had lit the first one on Tara Hill. In AD 433, St Patrick showed an acute understanding of symbolism when he lit a fire on Slane Hill, ten miles from Tara, *before* the High King Laoghaire lit his; he could not have made a more dramatic claim to the usurpation of spiritual leadership over the whole island. St David made a similar historic gesture in Wales in the following century.

Incidentally, much of the symbolism of Tara as the spiritual focus of ancient Ireland is immediately recognizable to anyone who has worked in a Magic Circle. Tara is in Meath (*Midhe*, 'centre') and was the seat of the High Kings; its ground-plan is still visible as great twin circular earthworks. Tara's ritual Banqueting Hall had a central hall for the High King himself, surrounded by four inward-facing halls which were allotted to the four provincial kingdoms: to the North for Ulster, to the East for Leinster, to the South for Munster, and to the West for Connacht. That is why the four provinces are traditionally

---

2. There is always overlap. The Cerne Abbas giant cut in the Dorset turf is a Baal figure, as shown by his Herculean club and phallus, and his local name, Helith, is clearly the Greek *helios* (Sun); yet 'Cerne' is equally clearly Cernunnos. And Baal Hammon of Carthage was also a true Baal or Bel (his Great Mother consort was named Tanit—cf. the Irish Dana and the Welsh Don); yet he was horned.

known as 'fifths', because of the vital Centre which completes them, as Spirit completes and integrates Earth, Air, Fire and Water. Even the elemental ritual tools are represented, in the Four Treasures of the Tuatha Dé Danann: the Stone of Fál (Destiny) which cried aloud when the rightful High King sat on it, the Sword and Spear of Lugh, and the Cauldron of the Dagda (the Father God).

All four were male symbols, as one might expect in a warrior society; but the archetypal matrilinear foundations still shone through at the inauguration of a lesser king, ruler of a *tuath* or tribe. This was "a symbolic marriage with Sovereignty, a fertility rite for which the technical term was *banais rígi* 'royal wedding'". The same used to be true of the High Kings: "The legendary Queen Medb, whose name means 'intoxication', was originally a personification of sovereignty, for we are told that she was the wife of nine kings of Ireland, and elsewhere that only one who was mated with her could be king. Of King Cormac it was said . . . 'until Medb slept with the lad, Cormac was not king of Ireland.' " (Dillon and Chadwick, *The Celtic Realms*, p. 125.)

It is easy to see, then, why Tara had to be the igniting-point for the community's regenerative Bel-fire; and the same would have been true of the corresponding spiritual foci in other lands. Ireland merely happens to be the country where the details of the tradition have been most clearly preserved.

(On the whole complex symbolism of Tara, the Reeses' *Celtic Heritage* makes fascinating reading for witches and occultists.)

A feature of the Bealtaine fire festival in many lands was jumping over the fire. (We say 'was', but in discussing seasonal folk-customs the past tense seldom proves to be entirely justified.) Young people jumped it to bring themselves husbands or wives; intending travellers to ensure a safe journey; pregnant women to ensure an easy delivery, and so on. Cattle were driven through its ashes—or between two such fires—to ensure a good milk-yield. The magical properties of the festival fire form a persistent belief, as we shall also see under Midsummer, Samhain and Yule. (Both Scottish and Irish Gaelic, incidentally, have a saying 'caught between two Bealtaine fires', meaning 'caught in a dilemma'.)

Talking of cattle—next day, 1st May, was an important one

in old Ireland. On that day the women, children and herdsmen took the cattle off to the summer pastures, or 'booleys' (*buaile* or *buailte*), until Samhain. The same thing still happens, on the same dates, in the Alps and other parts of Europe. Another Irish (and Scottish) Gaelic word for summer pasture is *áiridh*; and Doreen Valiente suggests (*Witchcraft for Tomorrow*, p. 164) that "there is just a chance that the name 'Aradia' is Celtic in origin," connected with this word. In North Italian witchcraft, which, as Leland (see Bibliography) has shown, derives from Etruscan roots, Aradia is the daughter of Diana (or, as the Etruscans themselves called her, Aritimi, a variant of the Greek Artemis). The Etruscans flourished in Tuscany from about the eighth to the fourth century BC, till the Romans conquered the last of their city-states, Volsinii, in 280 BC. From the fifth century onwards, they had much contact with the Gaulish Celts, sometimes as enemies and sometimes as allies; so it may very well be that the Celts brought Aradia there. 'Daughter', in the development of pantheons, often means 'later version'—and in the Aradia legend, Aradia learned much of her wisdom from her mother, which would tally with the undoubted fact that the brilliant Etruscan civilization was admired and envied by their Celtic neighbours. It is interesting that, in both Irish and Scottish, *áiridh* or a slight variant of it also means 'worth, merit'.

And in case anyone thinks that Aradia reached Britain only through Leland's nineteenth-century researches—in the form 'Herodias', she appears as an English witch-goddess name in the tenth-century *Canon Episcopi*.

Back to Bealtaine itself. Oak is the tree of the God of the Waxing Year; hawthorn, at this season, is a tree of the White Goddess. The strong folklore taboo on breaking hawthorn branches or bringing them into the house is traditionally lifted on May Eve, when sprigs of it may be cut for the Goddess's festival. (Irish farmers, and even earth-moving roadbuilders, are still reluctant to cut down lone hawthorns; a 'fairy' hawthorn stood by itself in the middle of a pasture of the farm we lived on at Ferns, County Wexford, and similar respected examples can be seen all over the country.)

However, if you want blossoms for your ritual (for example, as chaplets in the women witches' hair), you cannot be certain of finding hawthorn in flower as early as May Eve, and you will probably have to be content with the young leaves. Our own solution is to use blackthorn, whose flowers appear in April, ahead of the leaves. Blackthorn (sloe) is also a Goddess tree at this season—but it belongs to the Goddess in her dark, devouring aspect, as the bitterness of its autumn fruit would suggest. It used to be regarded as 'the witches' tree'—in the malevolent sense—and unlucky. But to fear the dark aspect of the Goddess is to miss the truth that she consumes only to give new birth. If the Mysteries could be summed up in one sentence, it might be this: "At the core of the Bright Mother is the Dark Mother, and at the core of the Dark Mother is the Bright Mother." The sacrifice-and-rebirth theme of our Bealtaine ritual reflects this truth, so, to symbolize the two aspects in balance, our women wear hawthorn in leaf and blackthorn in blossom, intertwined.

Another taboo lifted on May Eve was the early British one on hunting the hare. The hare, as well as being a Moon animal, has a fine reputation for randiness and fecundity; so has the goat, and both figure in the sacrificial aspect of the May Day fertility traditions. The Love Chase is a widespread form of this tradition; it underlies the Lady Godiva legend and that of the Teutonic goddess Eostre or Ostara after whom Easter is named, as well as such folk-festivals as the May Day 'Obby Oss' ceremony in Padstow, Cornwall. (On the alluring and mysterious figure of the love-chase woman "neither clothed nor unclothed, neither on foot nor on horseback, neither on water nor on dry land, neither with nor without a gift", who is "easily recognized as the May-Eve aspect of the Love-and-Death goddess," see Graves, *The White Goddess*, p. 403 onwards.)

But apart from—or rather, in amplification of—the enactment of these Goddess and God-King mysteries, Bealtaine for ordinary people was a festival of unashamed human sexuality and fertility. Maypole, nuts and 'the gown of green' were frank symbols of penis, testicles and the covering of a woman by a man. Dancing round the maypole, hunting for nuts in the woods, 'greenwood marriages' and staying up all night to watch the May sun rise, were unequivocal activities, which is why the Puritans suppressed them with such pious horror. (Parliament made maypoles illegal in 1644, but they came back with the

Restoration; in 1661 a 134-foot maypole was set up in the Strand.)

Robin Hood, Maid Marian and Little John played a big part in May Day folklore; and many people with surnames such as Hodson, Robinson, Jenkinson, Johnson and Godkin owe their ancestry to some distant May Eve in the woods.

Branches and flowers used to be brought back from the woods on May morning to decorate the village's doors and windows, and young people would carry garlands in procession, singing. The garlands were usually of intersecting hoops. Sir J. G. Frazer wrote at the beginning of this century: "It appears that a hoop wreathed with rowan and marsh marigold, and bearing suspended within it two balls, is still carried on May Day by villagers in some parts of Ireland. The balls, which are sometimes covered with gold and silver paper, are said to have originally represented the sun and moon." (*The Golden Bough*, p. 159.) Maybe—but Frazer, splendid pioneer though he was, often seemed to be (or, in the climate of his time, discreetly pretended to be) blind to sexual symbolism.

Another May morning custom in Ireland was 'skimming the wells'. You went to the well of a prosperous neighbour (presumably before he was up and about) and skimmed the surface of the water, to acquire his luck for yourself. In another variant of this custom, you skimmed your own well, to ensure a good butter-yield for the year—and also, one may guess, to forestall any neighbour who was after *your* luck.

Folk-memory survives in curious ways. A Dublin friend—a good Catholic in his fifties—tells us that when he was a boy in north County Longford, his father and mother used to take the children out at midnight on May Eve, and the whole family would dance naked in the young crops. The explanation the children were given was that this would protect them against catching colds for the next twelve months; but it would be interesting to know whether the parents themselves believed this to be the true reason or were really concerned with the fertility of the crops and were giving the children a 'respectable' explanation in case they talked—particularly in the priest's hearing. Our friend also tells us that the crops were always sown by 25th March to ensure a good harvest; and 25th March used to be regarded as the Spring Equinox (compare

25th December for Christmas instead of the astronomically exact solstice).

"One of the most widespread superstitions in England held that washing the face in May morning dew would beautify the skin," the *Encyclopaedia Britannica* says. "Pepys alludes to the practice in his *Diary*, and as late as 1791 a London newspaper reported that 'yesterday, being the first of May, a number of persons went into the fields and bathed their faces with the dew on the grass with the idea that it would render them beautiful.'" Ireland has the same tradition.

But to return to the greenwood. Today, over-population and not under-population is humanity's problem; and more enlightened attitudes to sexual relationships (though still developing unevenly) would hardly be compatible with the greenwood-orgy method of producing a new crop of Hodsons and Godkins. But both the cheerful frankness and the dark mystery can and should be expressed. That is what the Sabbats are all about.

In our Bealtaine rite, we have woven as much as we could of the traditional symbolism, short of overloading it and blunting its edge with obscurity—or, worse, taking the fun out of it. We leave it to the reader to discern the weaving. But perhaps it is worth mentioning that the High Priest's declamation, "*I am a stag of seven times*," etc., consists of those lines of the Song of Amergin which belong, according to Robert Graves's allocation, to the seven tree-months in the Oak King's cycle.

We have added one quite separate little rite which was suggested to us by reading Ovid's *Fasti*. On 1st May, the Romans paid homage to their Lares, or household gods; and it seemed appropriate for us to do the same on the night when the Bel-fire is extinguished and rekindled. All homes, to be honest, possess objects which are in effect Lares. Ours include a foot-high Venus de Milo acquired by Stewart's parents before he was born; slightly battered, twice broken in two and mended, she has come to be a much-loved Guardian of the Home and a true Lar. She now smiles Hellenistically down on our Bealtaine rites. Other witches may also feel that this little annual homage is a pleasant custom to adopt.

The Preparation

The cauldron is placed in the centre of the Circle, with a candle burning inside it; this represents the Bel-fire.

Sprigs of hawthorn and blackthorn decorate the altar, and chaplets of the two combined (with the thorns clipped off) are made for the women witches. (A shot of hair-spray on the blossoms beforehand will help to prevent the petals falling.) The hawthorn and blackthorn should be gathered on May Eve itself, and it is customary to apologize and explain to each tree as you cut it.

If oak leaves can be found at this season in your area, a chaplet of them is made for the High Priest, in his role as Oak King. (A permanent oak crown is a useful coven accessory—see under Yule, p. 145.)

A green scarf, or piece of gauze, at least a yard square, is laid by the altar.

As many wax tapers as there are people in the coven are placed close to the cauldron.

The 'cakes' for consecration on this occasion should be a bowl of nuts.

If you are including the rite for the Guardian of the House, this (or these) are placed on the edge of the Circle near the East candle, with one or two joss-sticks in a holder ready for lighting at the appropriate moment. (If your Guardian is not movable, a symbol of it may stand in its place; for example, if it is a tree in your garden, bring in a sprig of it—again with the appropriate apology and explanation.)

The Ritual

After the Witches' Rune, the coven spread themselves around the Circle area between the cauldron and the perimeter and start a soft, rhythmic clapping.

The High Priest picks up the green scarf, gathers it lengthwise like a rope and holds it with one end in each hand. He starts to move towards the High Priestess, making as though to throw the scarf over her shoulders and pull her to him; but she backs away from him, tantalizingly.

While the coven continue their rhythmic clapping, the High Priestess continues to elude the pursuing High Priest. She beckons to him and teases him but always steps back before he can capture her with the scarf. She weaves in and out of the coven, and the other women step in the High Priest's way to help her elude him.

After a while, say after two or three 'laps' of the Circle, the High Priestess allows the High Priest to capture her by throwing the scarf over her head to behind her shoulders and pulling her to him. They kiss and separate, and the High Priest hands the scarf to another man.

The other man then pursues *his* partner, who eludes him, beckons to him and teases him in exactly the same way; the clapping goes on all the time. (See Plate 12.) After a while she, too, allows herself to be captured and kissed.

The man then hands the scarf to another man, and the pursuit-game continues until every couple in the coven has taken part.

The last man hands the scarf back to the High Priest.

Once again the High Priest pursues the High Priestess; but this time the pace is much slower, almost stately, and her eluding and beckoning more solemn, as though she is tempting him into danger; and this time the others do not intervene. The pursuit continues until the High Priestess places herself between the cauldron and the altar, facing the altar and two or three paces from it. Then the High Priest halts with his back to the altar and captures her with the scarf.

They embrace solemnly but wholeheartedly; but after a few seconds of the kiss, the High Priest lets the scarf fall from his hands, and the High Priestess releases him and takes a step backwards.

The High Priest drops to his knees, sits back on his heels and lowers his head, chin on chest.

The High Priestess spreads her arms, signalling for the clapping to stop. She then calls forward two women by name and places them on each side of the High Priest, facing inwards, so that the three tower over him. The High Priestess picks up the scarf, and the three of them spread it between them over the High Priest. They lower it slowly and then release it, so that it covers his head like a shroud.

The High Priestess sends the two women back to their places and calls forward two men by name. She instructs them to extinguish the two altar candles (*not* the Earth candle), and when they have done so, she sends them back to their places.

The High Priestess then turns and kneels close to the cauldron, facing it. She gestures to the rest of the coven to kneel around the cauldron with her.

Only the High Priest stays where he is in front of the altar, kneeling but 'dead'.

When everyone is in place, the High Priestess blows out the candle in the cauldron and is silent for a moment. Then she says:

"The Bel-fire is extinguished, and the Oak King is dead. He has embraced the Great Mother and died of his love; so has it been, year by year, since time began. Yet if the Oak King is dead—he who is the God of the Waxing Year—all is dead; the fields bear no crops, the trees bear no fruit, and the creatures of the Great Mother bear no young. What shall we do, therefore, that the Oak King may live again?"

The coven reply:

"Re-kindle the Bel-fire!"

The High Priestess says:

"So mote it be."

The High Priestess takes a taper, rises, goes to the altar, lights the taper from the Earth candle and kneels again at the cauldron. She relights the cauldron candle with her taper. (See Plate 7.) Then she says:

"Take each of you a taper and light it from the Bel-fire."

The coven do so; and finally the High Priestess lights a second taper for herself. Summoning the original two women to accompany her, she rises and turns to face the High Priest. She gestures to the two women to lift the scarf from the High Priest's head; they do so (see Plate 8) and lay it on the floor.

The High Priestess sends the two women back to their places and summons the two men. She instructs them to relight the altar candles with their tapers. When they have done so, she sends them back to their places.

She then holds out one of her tapers to the High Priest (who so far has not moved) and says:

"Come back to us, Oak King, that the land may be fruitful."

The High Priest rises, and accepts the taper. He says:

"I am a stag of seven tines;
I am a wide flood on a plain;
I am a wind on the deep waters;
I am a shining tear of the sun;
I am a hawk on a cliff;
I am fair among flowers;
I am a god who sets the head afire with smoke."

The High Priestess and High Priest lead a ring dance around the cauldron, the rest of the coven following, all carrying their tapers. The mood becomes joyous. As they dance, they chant:

"Oh, do not tell the Priest of our Art,
Or he would call it a sin;
But we shall be out in the woods all night,
A-conjuring Summer in!
And we bring you news by word of mouth
For women, cattle and corn—
Now is the Sun come up from the South
With Oak, and Ash, and Thorn!"[3]

They repeat *"With Oak, and Ash, and Thorn"* ad lib., till the High Priestess blows out her taper and lays it by the cauldron. The rest do the same. Then the entire coven link hands and circle faster and faster. Every now and then the High Priestess calls a name, or a couple's names, and whoever is called breaks away, jumps the cauldron and rejoins the ring. When all have jumped, the High Priestess cries *"Down!"* and everybody sits.

That, apart from the Great Rite, is the end of the Bealtaine ritual; but if the Guardian of the House is to be honoured, it is most suitably done while the rest of the coven are relaxing. The Guardian ritual is of course performed by the couple, or individual, in whose house the Sabbat is being held—who may or may not be the High Priestess and High Priest. If it is an

---

3. This (the only substantial item in the Book of Shadows' Bealtaine ritual) is a slightly altered version of verse 5 of Rudyard Kipling's poem *A Tree Song*, from the "Weland's Sword" story in *Puck of Pook's Hill*. It is one of Gerald Gardner's happier borrowings, and we are sure the shade of Kipling does not mind.

individual, his or her working partner will assist; if he or she is unpartnered, the High Priestess or High Priest may do so.

The couple approach the East candle, while the rest of the coven remain seated but turn to face East with them.

One of the couple lights the joss-sticks in front of the Guardian, while the other says:

"Guardian of this House, watch over it in the year to come, till again the Bel-fire is extinguished and relit. Bless this house, and be blessed by it; let all who live here, and all friends who are welcomed here, prosper under this roof. So mote it be!"

All say:

"So mote it be!"

The couple rejoin the coven.

Bealtaine and Samhain are traditional 'Mischief Nights'—what Doreen Valiente has called "the in-between times, when the year was swinging on its hinges, the doors of the Other World were open, and anything could happen". So when all is done, the Great Rite celebrated, and the wine and nuts shared, this is the night for forfeits. In imposing bizarre little tasks or ordeals, the High Priestess's inventiveness may run wild—always remembering, of course, that it is the High Priest's final privilege to devise a forfeit for *her*.

One final point; if you are holding your Bealtaine festival outdoors, the Bel-fire which is lit should be a bonfire. This should be laid ready with kindling which will catch quickly. But the *old* Bel-fire which the High Priestess extinguishes should be a candle, protected if necessary inside a lantern. It would not be practicable, unless the Sabbat were a large-scale affair, to extinguish a bonfire in the middle of the ritual.

If you live in an area where witchcraft activity is known and respected—or at least tolerated—and have the use of a hilltop, the sudden blazing up of a Bealtaine fire in the darkness may stir some interesting folk-memories.

But if you do light a bonfire—on this or any other occasion, have a fire-extinguisher ready to hand in case of emergency. Witches who start heath-fires or woodland-fires will quickly lose any local respect they may have built up; and quite right too.

VII Midsummer, 22nd June

The Sun-God significance of the Midsummer Sabbat is, literally, as clear as day. At the Summer Solstice, he is at his highest and brightest, and his day is at its longest. Witches, naturally and rightly, greet and honour him at the peak of his annual cycle, invoking him to "put to flight the powers of darkness" and to bring fertility to the land. Midsummer is perhaps the most celebratory of the Festivals, in the sense that it rejoices in the full flood of the year's abundance, the apogee of light and warmth.

But the Sabbat cycle, even at the height of its joy, always takes into account what lies behind and before. As the ancient Greeks put it: *"Panta rhei, ouden menei"*[1]—"Everything flows,

1. πάντα ρεῖ οὐδὲν μένει—Heraclitus, c.513BC.

nothing is static." Life is a process, not a state; and the witches' Sabbats are essentially a means of putting oneself in tune with that process.

So at Midsummer, the 'process' aspect is reflected in the other God-theme—that of the Oak King and Holly King. At Midsummer, the Oak King, God of the Waxing Year, falls to the Holly King, his twin, the God of the Waning Year, because the blazing peak of summer is also, by its very nature, the beginning of the Holly King's reign, with its inexorable progression to the dark nadir of midwinter, when he in turn will die at the hands of the reborn Oak King.

The Oak King's midsummer death has taken many forms in mythology. He was burned alive, or blinded with a mistletoe stake, or crucified on a T-shaped cross; and in ancient times the human enactor of the Oak King was thus sacrificed in actuality. His death was followed by a seven-day wake. But the Oak King himself, as God of the Waxing Year, withdrew to the circumpolar stars, the Corona Borealis, the Celtic Caer Arianrhod— that turning wheel of the heavens which the ancient Egyptians called *ikhem-sek*, 'not-knowing-destruction', because its stars never dipped below the horizon even at midwinter. Here he awaited his equally inevitable rebirth.

Robert Graves suggests that the biblical story of Samson (a folk-hero of the Oak King type) reflects this pattern: after being shorn of his power, he is blinded and sent to serve in a turning mill. (One might also suggest that Delilah, who presides over his downfall, represents the Goddess as Death-in-Life and that, in demoting her to villainess, Hebrew patriarchalism forgot or suppressed the sequel—that in due course, as Life-in-Death, she would be destined to preside over his restoration.)

Graves points out, further, that "since in mediaeval practice St John the Baptist, who lost his head on St John's Day" (24th June), "took over the Oak King's title and customs, it was natural to let Jesus, as John's merciful successor, take over the Holly King. . . . 'Of all the trees that are in the wood, the holly bears the crown'. . . . The identification of the pacific Jesus with the holly or holly-oak must be regretted as poetically inept, except in so far as he declared that he had come to bring not peace but the sword." (*The White Goddess*, pp. 180–1.)

Any significant Midsummer Sabbat ritual must embrace both

these God-themes, for the solstices are key points on both. But what of the Goddess? What is her role in the Midsummer drama?

The Goddess, as we have pointed out, is unlike the God in that she never undergoes death and rebirth. In fact, she never changes—she merely presents different faces. At the Winter Solstice she shows her Life-in-Death aspect; though her Earth-body seems cold and still, yet she gives birth to the new Sun-God and presides over the replacement of Holly King by Oak King with his promise of resurgent life. At the Summer Solstice she shows her Death-in-Life aspect; her Earth-body is exuberantly fecund and sensuous, greeting her Sun-God consort at the zenith of his powers—yet she knows it is a transient zenith, and at the same time she presides over the death of the Oak King and the enthronement of his dark (but necessary, and thus not evil) twin. At Midsummer the Goddess dances her magnificent Dance of Life; but even as she dances, she whispers to us: *"Panta rhei, ouden menei."*

Midsummer is both a fire festival and a water festival, the fire being the God-aspect and the water the Goddess-aspect, as the ritual should make clear. Midsummer is also sometimes called Beltane, because bonfires are lit as they are on May Eve; it has been suggested that St Patrick was largely responsible for this in Ireland, because he shifted Ireland's 'bonfire night' to St John's Eve to play down the pagan implications of May Eve.[2] He may

---

2. Throughout most of Ireland, the night for the communal Midsummer fire is 23rd June, the eve of St John's Day. But in some places it is traditionally 28th June, the eve of St Peter and St Paul's Day, sometimes known as 'Little Bonfire Night'. We have been unable to pin down the reason for this curious difference, but it might possibly have something to do with the old Julian calendar. In 1582 Pope Gregory XIII wiped out ten days to make the calendar astronomically correct, and it is the Gregorian calendar which the world still uses today. (It was not adopted by England, Scotland and Wales till 1752—by which time eleven days had to be dropped—and was general in Ireland by 1782.) But it is noticeable in many parts of Europe that old folk-customs which have escaped official Christian take-over tend to be pegged to the old calendar (see, for example, p. 124). St Peter and Paul is nearer to the Midsummer Solstice than St John *if the Gregorian reform is ignored*. So perhaps a stubborn pagan custom, which did in places ignore that reform, was there merely attached to the nearest important saint's day to make it as respectable as could be managed.

indeed have shifted the emphasis, but he can hardly have shifted the name, because Bealtaine *means* May in Irish; the use of the name for Midsummer can have arisen only in non-Gaelic-speaking countries.

In any case, Midsummer was a principal fire festival throughout Europe, and even among the Arabs and Berbers of North Africa; it was lesser, and late-developing, in the Celtic countries because they were not originally or naturally solar-oriented. Many of the customs have survived into modern times and often involve the turning, or rolling downhill, of a flaming wheel as a solar symbol. As at Bealtaine and Samhain (indeed, at every Festival) the bonfire itself has always been regarded as having great magical power. We have already mentioned (under Bealtaine) the custom of jumping the fire and driving cattle through it. Ashes from it were also scattered on the fields. In Ireland a burnt sod from the St John's Eve fire was a protective charm. In flax-growing countries the height achieved in jumping the fire was believed to foretell the height to which the flax would grow. Moroccans rubbed a paste of the ashes into their hair to prevent baldness. Another custom widespread throughout Europe was to strengthen the eyes by looking at the fire through bunches of larkspur or other flowers held in the hand.

Chapter LXII of Frazer's *Golden Bough* is a mine of information on fire-festival traditions.

For modern witches, fire is a central feature of the Midsummer Sabbat as it is of Bealtaine. But since the cauldron (which on May Eve holds the Bealtaine fire) is used at Midsummer for the water with which the High Priestess sprinkles her coven—and is referred to as 'the cauldron of Cerridwen', reaffirming its Goddess symbolism—we have drawn on another long-standing tradition by suggesting twin bonfires for the Midsummer rite (or twin candles as their equivalent if the festival is indoors). Magically, passing *between* them is regarded as the same as passing *over* a single fire and, if you are driving cattle through as a spell for a good milk-yield, is obviously more practical!

Of all the Sabbats, Midsummer in temperate climates is the one to hold out of doors if facilities and privacy permit; for skyclad observance, it and Lughnasadh may prove to be the

1. The Altar

2. (*Overleaf*) The Opening Ritual: Consecrating the Water and Salt

3. (*Overleaf, right*), Consecrating the Cakes

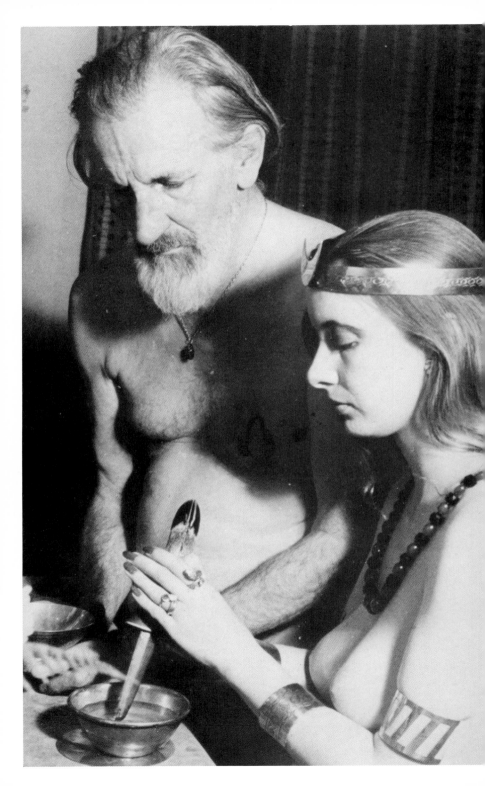

4. The Great Rite: "Assist me to erect the ancient altar"
5. Imbolg: The Triple Goddess – Maid, Mother and Crone

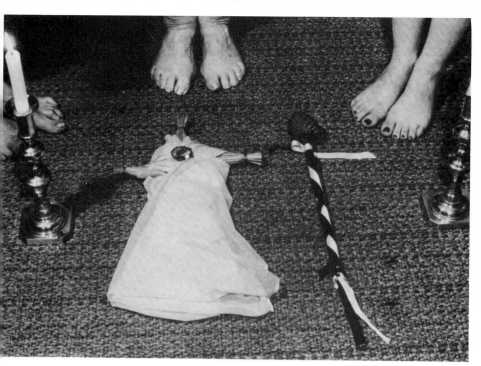

6. Imbolg: Brigid's Bed
7. Bealtaine: "Re-kindle the Bel-fire!"

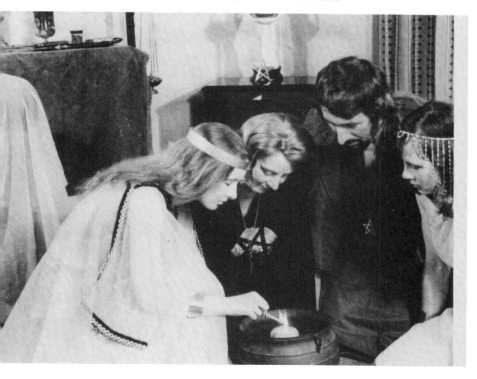

8. Bealtaine: Re-birth of the Oak King

9. (*Facing*) Midsummer: The Oak King has been vanquished by the Holly King, and the Goddess performs her Midsummer Dance to the Sun

10. The Wand and the Scourge held in the 'Osiris Position'

11. When privacy permits, outdoor rituals are better

12. Lughnasadh and Bealtaine: The Love Chase
13. (*Facing*) Lughnasadh: The Corn Dance
14. (*Below*) Autumn Equinox: "Behold the mystery"

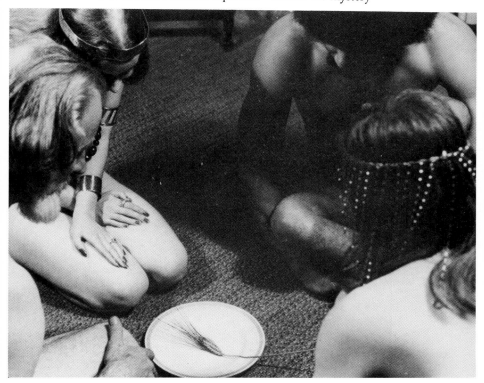

15. When a High Priestess has two more covens hived off from her own, she is entitled to call herself 'Witch Queen' and to wear the appropriate number of buckles on her witch's garter

16. Yule: The Goddess mourns the death of the Sun God

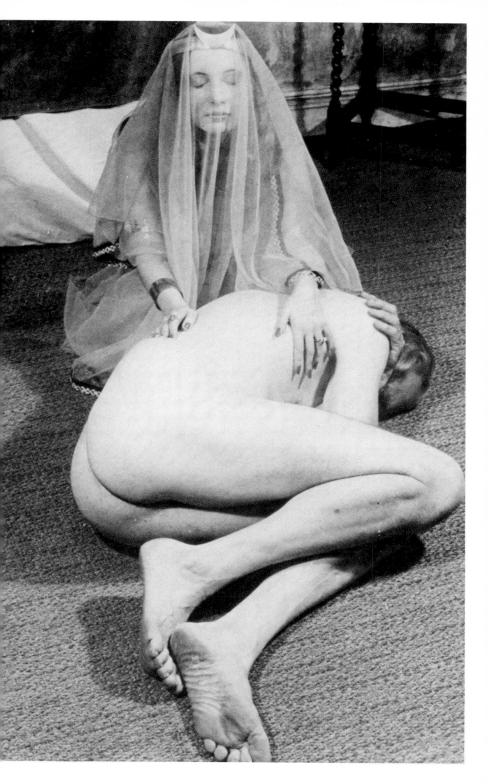

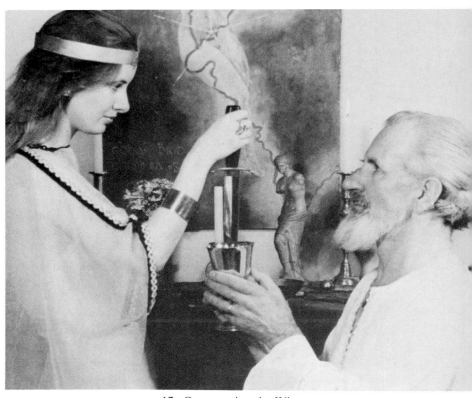

17. Consecrating the Wine

18. Sword and Athame symbolize the Fire element in our tradition.
Others attribute them to Air

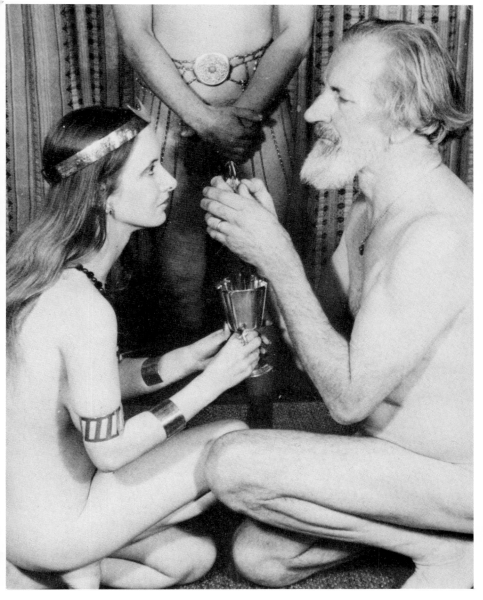

19. The symbolic Great Rite: "Here where the Lance and Grail unite"

20. (*Overleaf*) The Legend of the Descent of the Goddess: "Such was her beauty that Death himself knelt and laid his sword and crown at her feet"

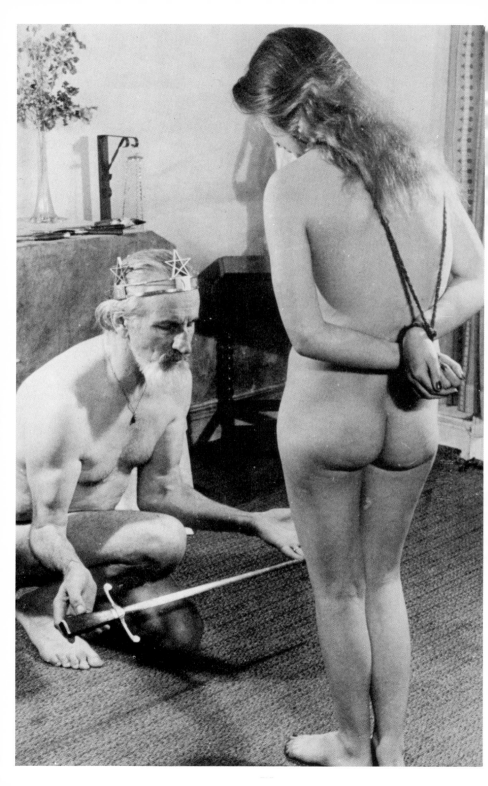

only ones. But as with the other Sabbats, we have described our ritual as for indoor celebration—if only because adaptation of an indoor 'script' to outdoor use is easier than the other way round.

Talking of skyclad—one Midsummer tradition may be of interest to any woman who is anxious to conceive and who owns a vegetable garden. She should walk through it naked on Midsummer Eve and also pluck some St John's Wort, if there is any. (If your vegetable garden is anything like ours, shoes might be thought a permissible modification of nakedness!) This is an intriguing mirror-image of the ancient and widespread fertility rite in which women walked naked round the fields to ensure an abundant harvest, often emphasizing their sympathetic magic by 'riding' (a discreet euphemism) phallic 'broomsticks'. (See p. 86 for a twentieth-century survival of this.)

The Preparation

The cauldron is placed immediately in front of the altar, with some water in it and decorated with flowers. A branch of heather is placed beside it, ready for the High Priestess to sprinkle water with. (Quite apart from this branch, heather is a good plant, symbolically, for Circle decorations on this night; red heather is the passionate flower of Midsummer, and white heather represents the moderating influence—will controlling or directing passion.)

Two crowns, one of oak leaves and one of holly leaves, are made and placed beside the altar. The High Priest (who represents the Sun God) should be crowned too, but from the start of the ritual; his crown should be gold-coloured, and he may add any other accessories or decorations which enhance the solar symbolism.

High Priestess and Maiden may wear chaplets of summer flowers.

The two altar candles, in their holders, may be used at the appropriate moment as the 'bonfires'; or two other candles in holders may be kept ready. Outdoors, of course, two small bonfires will be laid ready for quick lighting—one halfway between the centre of the Circle and the East candle, one halfway between the centre and the West candle. (The outdoor Circle will, of course, be much larger, leaving room to dance between and around the bonfires.)

A dark-coloured scarf is laid by the altar, ready to use as a blindfold.

A number of straws are laid on the altar—as many as there are men at the Sabbat, except for the High Priest. One of them is longer than the rest, and one shorter. (If the High Priestess, for her own reasons, decides to nominate the two Kings instead of drawing lots for them, the straws are of course not needed.)

The Ritual

After the Witches' Rune, the Maiden fetches the straws from the altar and holds them in her hand so that all the ends are protruding separately, but nobody can see which are the short and long ones. The High Priestess says:

"*Let the men draw lots.*"

Each man (except the High Priest) draws a straw from the Maiden's hand and shows it to the High Priestess. The High Priestess points to the man who has drawn the long straw and says:

"*Thou are the Oak King, God of the Waxing Year. Maiden, bring his crown!*"

The Maiden places the oak-leaf crown on the head of the Oak King.

The High Priestess points to the man who has drawn the short straw and says:

"*Thou art the Holly King, God of the Waning Year. Maiden, bring his crown!*"

The Maiden places the holly-leaf crown on the head of the Holly King.

The High Priestess leads the Oak King to the centre of the Circle, where he stands facing West. The rest of the coven surround him, facing inwards, except for the High Priestess and High Priest, who stand with their backs to the altar on either side of the cauldron.

The High Priestess says:

"*With the Sun God at the height of his power and majesty, the waxing of the year is accomplished, and the reign of the Oak King is ended. With the Sun God at the height of his splendour, the waning of the year begins; the Holly King must slay his brother the Oak King, and rule over my land until the depth of winter, when his brother shall be born again.*"

The Holly King moves in front of the Oak King, facing him, and places his hands on the Oak King's shoulders, pressing downwards. The Oak King falls to his knees. Meanwhile the Maiden fetches the scarf, and she and the Holly King blindfold the Oak King. The rest of the coven move back to the perimeter of the Circle and sit down, facing inwards.

The High Priestess picks up her athame and moves forward;[3] the Holly King takes her place before the altar, on the other side of the cauldron from the High Priest. The High Priestess, athame in hand, dances deosil around the kneeling Oak King (see Plate 9) while the High Priest declaims the following poem, steadily and clearly, emphasizing the beat and maintaining the rhythm:

> "*Dance, Lady, dance—on the Oak King's tomb,*
> *Where he lies half a year in thy quiet womb.*
>
> *Dance, Lady, dance—at the Holly King's birth,*
> *Who has slain his twin for the love of Earth.*
>
> *Dance, Lady, dance—to the Sun God's power*
> *And his touch of gold on field and flower.*
>
> *Dance, Lady, dance—with thy blade in hand,*
> *That shall summon the Sun to bless thy land.*
>
> *Dance, Lady, dance—in the Silver Wheel,*
> *Where the Oak King rests, his wounds to heal.*
>
> *Dance, Lady, dance—for the Holly King's reign,*
> *Till his brother the Oak shall rise again.*
>
> *Dance, Lady, dance—in the moonlit sky*
> *To the Threefold Name men know thee by.*
>
> *Dance, Lady, dance—on the turning Earth*
> *For the Birth that is Death, and the Death that is Birth.*
>
> *Dance, Lady, dance—to the Sun on high,*
> *For his burning splendour, too, must die.*
>
> *Dance, Lady, dance—to the year's long tide,*
> *For through all change must thou abide.*"

---

3. It is symbolically fitting that the High Priestess, representing the Goddess, should perform the Midsummer Dance; but if she feels that one of her other women witches is a particularly talented dancer and would do it more effectively, she may delegate the task to her.

—and now, accelerating the rhythm—

> "*Dance for the Sun in glory,*
> *Dance for the Oak King's passing,*
> *Dance for the Holly King's triumph—*
> *Dance, Lady, dance—*
> *Dance, Lady, dance—*
> *Dance, Lady, dance . . .*"

The coven join in the chant "*Dance, Lady, dance,*" to a fast insistent beat, till the High Priest signals to them to stop and also stops himself.

The High Priestess ends her dance by laying down her athame on the altar. She and the Maiden help the Oak King to rise, and they lead him, still blindfold, to kneel before the West candle.

The High Priest then says:

"*The spirit of the Oak King is gone from us, to rest in Caer Arianrhod, the Castle of the Silver Wheel; until, with the turning of the year, the season shall come when he shall return to rule again. The spirit is gone; therefore let the man among us who has stood for that spirit be freed from his task.*"

The Maiden removes the Oak King's blindfold, and the High Priestess removes his oak-leaf crown. They lay them on each side of the West candle and then help the man rise; he turns and again becomes a part of the coven.

The High Priest says:

"*Let the Midsummer fires shine forth!*"

The Maiden and the Holly King fetch the two altar candles and place them on the East-West line, equidistant from the centre and four or five feet apart. Meanwhile the High Priestess rejoins the High Priest at the altar. (Outdoors, Maiden and Holly King light the two bonfires.)

The Maiden then fetches the High Priest's athame from the altar and stands beside the westerly midsummer candle, facing East. The Holly King fetches the chalice of wine and stands beside the easterly midsummer candle, facing West.

The symbolic Great Rite is then enacted by the High Priestess and High Priest—the High Priestess placing herself between the two candles, and the Maiden and Holly King handing over the athame and chalice at the appropriate moment.

After the Great Rite and the passing of the chalice, the High Priest stands before the altar with the wand in his right hand and the scourge in his left, crossed over his breast in the Osiris Position. The High Priestess faces him, and invokes joyfully:[4]

"Great One of Heaven, Power of the Sun, we invoke thee in thine ancient names—Michael, Balin, Arthur, Lugh; come again as of old into this thy land. Lift up thy shining spear of light to protect us. Put to flight the powers of darkness. Give us fair woodlands and green fields, blossoming orchards and ripening corn. Bring us to stand upon thy hill of vision and show us the path to the lovely realms of the Gods."

She then traces the Invoking Pentagram of Earth in front of the High Priest with her right forefinger. The High Priest raises both his hands high and then plunges the wand into the water in the cauldron. He then holds it up, saying:

"The Spear to the Cauldron, the Lance to the Grail, Spirit to Flesh, Man to Woman, Sun to Earth."

The High Priest lays the wand and scourge down on the altar and joins the rest of the coven. The High Priestess picks up the heather branch and stands by the cauldron. She says:

"Dance ye before the Cauldron of Cerridwen, the Goddess, and be ye blessed with the touch of this consecrated water; even as the Sun, the Lord of Life, ariseth in his strength in the sign of the Waters of Life!"

The coven, led by the High Priest, start to move deosil round the Circle, outside the two candles. As each person passes her, the High Priestess sprinkles him or her with water with her heather branch. When she has sprinkled everybody, she joins the moving ring.

The High Priestess then orders everybody in turn—singly or in couples—to pass between the midsummer candles and to wish as they go. When everyone has been through, the High Priestess and High Priest pass through together. They then turn back and pick up the two candles and return them to the altar, to leave room for the dance.

High Priestess and High Priest then lead the coven in spontaneous and joyous dancing, until the High Priestess decides it is time for the party stage of the Sabbat.

---

4. Written by Doreen Valiente, down to "Waters of Life".

VIII   Lughnasadh, 31st July

Lughnasadh (pronounced '*loo*-nus-uh') means 'the commemoration of Lugh'. In its simplified spelling, *Lúnasa*, it is Irish Gaelic for the month of August. As *Lunasda* or *Lunasdal* ('*loo*-nus-duh', '-dul'), it is Scottish Gaelic for Lammas, 1st August; and the Manx equivalent is *Laa Luanys* or *Laa Lunys*. In Scotland, the period from a fortnight before Lunasda to a fortnight after is known as Iuchar, while in the Dingle Peninsula of County Kerry the second fortnight is known as *An Lughna Dubh* (the dark Lugh-festival)—suggesting "that they are echoes of a lunar reckoning whereby Lughnasa would have been celebrated in conjunction with a phase of the moon" (Máire MacNeill, *The Festival of Lughnasa*, p. 16).

Throughout the British Isles (not only in the 'Celtic fringe' but also in such places as County Durham and Yorkshire),

Lughnasadh folk-customs have attached themselves almost entirely to the Sunday before or the Sunday after 1st August— not merely through Christianization but because they involved large gatherings of people, often on mountains or high hills, which were possible only on the days of leisure which Christianity had conveniently provided.

Of the Lughnasadh survivals in these islands, Ireland supplies a veritable gold-mine, partly because, as we have already pointed out, in Ireland rural culture has been far less eroded by urban culture than elsewhere, but also for another historical reason. During the centuries when the Catholic religion was proscribed or persecuted, the Irish peasantry, deprived of their buildings of worship, clung all the more fervently to the open-air holy places which were all that was left to them. So, obeying an urge far older than Christianity, priests and people together climbed the sacred heights or sought out the magical wells, to mark those turning-points in Mother Earth's year which were too important to them to be unacknowledged merely because their churches were roofless or requisitioned by an alien creed. On such heights as Croagh Patrick, they still do; more of that later.

Máire MacNeill's book, quoted above, brings together an astonishing wealth of these survivals—seven hundred pages of customs, folklore and root-legend which should not be missed by any serious student of the Eight Festivals.

Who was Lugh? He was a fire- and light-god of the Baal/ Hercules type; his name may be from the same root as the Latin *lux*, meaning light (which also gives us Lucifer, 'the light-bringer'). He is really the same god as Baal/Beli/Balor, but a later and more sophisticated version of him. In mythology, the historical replacing of one god by a later form (following invasion, for example, or a revolutionary advance in technology) is often remembered as the killing, blinding or emasculation of the older by the younger, while the essential continuity is acknowledged by making the younger into the son or grandson of the elder. (If the superseded deity is a goddess, she often reappears as the wife of the newcomer.) Thus Lugh, in Irish legend, was a leader of the Tuatha Dé Danann ('the peoples of the Goddess Dana'), the last-but-one conquerors of Ireland in the mythological cycle, while Balor was king of the

Fomors, whom the Tuatha Dé defeated; and in the battle Lugh blinded Balor. Yet according to most versions, Balor was his grandfather, and Dana/Danu was Balor's wife. (In this case, marriage demoted Balor, not Dana.)

Other versions make Lugh Balor's son. The folklore of our own village does, apparently; as Máire MacNeill (*ibid.*, p. 408) records: "From Ballycroy in Mayo comes a saying proverbial in thunder-storms:

> '*Tá gaoth Lugha Lámhfhada ag eiteall anocht san aer.*'
> '*Seadh, agus drithleógai a athar. Balor Béimeann an t-athair.*'
> ('Lugh Long-arm's wind is flying in the air tonight.'
> 'Yes, and the sparks of his father, Balor Béimann.')"

Lugh, then, is Balor all over again—and certainly associated with a technological revolution. In the legend of the Tuatha Dé's victory, Lugh spares the life of Bres, a captured enemy leader, in exchange for advice on ploughing, sowing and reaping. "The story clearly contains a harvest myth in which the secret of agricultural prosperity is wrested from a powerful and reluctant god by Lugh" (MacNeill, *ibid.*, p. 5).

Lugh's superior cleverness and versatility is indicated by his titles *Lugh Lámhfhada* (pronounced 'loo law-*vaw*da') and *Samhioldánach* ('sawvil-*daw*noch', with the 'ch' as in 'loch'), "equally skilled in all the arts". His Welsh equivalent (grandson of Beli and Don) is Llew Llaw Gyffes, variously translated as "the lion with the steady hand" (Graves) and "the shining one with the skilful hand" (Gantz).

Significantly, Lugh is often the patron-deity of a town, such as Carlisle (Luguvalium), Lyon in France, Leyden in Holland and Legnica (German, Liegnitz) in Poland. Towns were alien to the earlier Celts; their first (Continental) towns were for commercial convenience in trading with the Mediterranean civilizations, from which they copied them; for strongpoints in exacting tribute from the trade-routes; or later, as a result of the absorption of Celtic Gaul into the patterns of the Roman Empire. Of the British Celts, a writer as late as Strabo (*c.* 55 BC–AD 25) could still say: "Their cities are the woods. They enclose a large area with felled trees and set up huts to house themselves and their animals, never with the intention of staying very long in these places." So by the time the Celts got

around to naming towns, Balor had been outshone by Lugh—
apart from the fact that a large proportion of the population of
those towns would be craftsmen, naturally devoted to Lugh
Samhioldánach.

Talking of take-overs—they happened of course with the
arrival of Christianity, too. A prime example is St Michael, who
was a later form of the Lucifer he 'defeated'. T. C. Lethbridge,
in *Witches: Investigating an Ancient Religion*, has shown how
many parish churches of St Michael coincide with places where
Lugh, the Celtic Lucifer or 'light-bringer', would have been
worshipped (pre-Reformation churches, that is; post-Reforma-
tion churchbuilders seem to have lost all sense of place-magic).[1]
And Michael, in magical tradition, rules the fire element.

That Lugh is also a type of the god who undergoes death and
rebirth in a sacrificial mating with the Goddess, is most clearly
seen in the legend of his Welsh manifestation, Llew Llaw
Gyffes. This story appears as part of *The Romance of Math the
Son of Mathonwy* in the *Mabinogion*; Graves gives Lady
Charlotte Guest's translation of it in *The White Goddess*.

Graves also says (*ibid.*, p. 178): "The Anglo-Saxon form of
Lughomass, mass in honour of the God Lugh or Llew, was
hlaf-mass, 'loaf-mass', with reference to the corn-harvest and
the killing of the Corn-king." The Tailltean Games, held in
Ireland at Lughnasadh, were orginally funeral-games, traditionally in honour of Lugh's dead foster-mother Tailte; but as
Graves points out (p. 302), this tradition "is late and mis-
leading". The wake-games were clearly to honour the sacrificed
Lugh himself. And unless one grasps the meaning of the
sacrificial-mating theme, one might be puzzled by the apparent
contradiction that an early Irish tradition also refers to the
wedding-feats of Lugh at Tailtiu; in a sense, this too is a
blurring of a half-remembered story, for he who mates with the
Goddess at harvest is already her Waning Year consort. As
Máire MacNeill rightly says (*ibid.*, p. 424): "Lughnasa, I would

---

1. On the whole subject of place-magic, not only of places of worship but also
(for example) of such things as Bealtaine fires, Tom Graves's *Needles of Stone* is
practically essential reading for witches who want not merely to feel but to
understand and experiment constructively with their relationship to Earth as a
living organism.

suggest, was one episode in the cycle of a divine marriage story but not necessarily the bridal time."

So in Lughnasadh we have the autumn parallel to the Bealtaine sacrificial mating with the God of the Waxing Year. On the human level, it is interesting that the Bealtaine 'greenwood marriages' were paralleled by the Lughnasadh 'Teltown marriages' (i.e., Tailltean), trial marriages which could be dissolved after a year and a day by the couple returning to the place where the union was celebrated and walking away from each other to North and South. (Wiccan handfasting has the same provision: the couple can dissolve it after a year and a day by returning to the High Priestess who handfasted them and informing her.) Teltown (modern Irish Tailteann, old Irish Tailtiu) is a village in County Meath, where tradition remembers a 'Hillock of the Bride-Price" and a 'Marriage Hollow'. The Tailltean Fair seems in later centuries to have become a mere marriage-market, with boys and girls kept apart till contracts were signed; but its origins must have been very different.

It stemmed, in fact, from the óenach, or tribal gathering, of pagan times—of which the óenach of Tailtiu was the most important, being associated with the High King, whose royal seat of Tara is only 15 miles away. (MacNeill, ibid., pp. 311–338.) These gatherings were a mixture of tribal business, horse-racing, athletic contests and ritual to ensure good fortune; and Lughnasadh was a favourite time for them. The Leinster óenach of Carman, the Wexford goddess (MacNeill, ibid., pp. 339–344), for example, was held on the banks of the River Barrow for the week beginning with the Lughnasadh feast, to secure for the tribe "corn and milk, mast and fish, and freedom from aggression by any outsider". (Gearóid Mac Niocaill, Ireland Before the Vikings, p. 49.) "Such deep-rooted traditions could not be jettisoned and had perforce to be tolerated and as far as possible Christianized. Thus in 784 the óenach of Teltown (Tailtiu) was sanctified by the relics of Erc of Slane." Mac Niocaill also says (p. 25) that Columcille—better known outside Ireland as St Columba—is credited with a bid to take over Lughnasadh "by converting it into a 'Feast of the Ploughmen', not apparently with any great success".

The ritual behaviour of the King, as the sacred personification of the tribe, was particularly important. At Lughnasadh, for example, the King of Tara's diet had to include fish from the Boyne, venison from Luibnech, bilberries from Brí Léith near Ardagh, and other obligatory items (Mac Niocaill, p. 47). (The bilberries are significant; see below.)

A formidable list of the taboos surrounding the Roman Sacred King, the Flamen Dialis, is given by Frazer (*The Golden Bough*, p. 230). Graves (*The White Goddess*, p. 130) points out what Frazer omits—that the Flamen, a Hercules-type figure, owed his position to his sacred marriage with the Flamenica; he could not divorce her, and if she died, he had to resign. It is the role of the Sacred King to bow to the Goddess-Queen.

This brings us straight back to Lughnasadh, for Graves goes on: "In Ireland this Hercules was named *Cenn Cruaich*, 'the Lord of the Mound', but after his supersession by a more benignant sacred king was remembered as *Cromm Cruaich* ('The Bowed One of the Mound')."

Crom Cruach (the usual modern spelling), also called Crom Dubh ('The Black Bowed One'), was a sacrificial god particularly associated with Lughnasadh; the last Sunday in July is still known as *Domhnach Chrom Dubh* ('Crom Dubh's Sunday') even though it has been Christianized. On that day every year, thousands of pilgrims climb Ireland's holy mountain, whose summit can be seen through our study window—the 2,510-foot Croagh Patrick (*Cruach Phádraig*) in County Mayo, where St Patrick is said to have fasted for forty days and defeated a host of demons.[2] The observance used to be a three-day one, starting on *Aoine Chrom Dubh*, the Friday preceding. It is still Ireland's most spectacular pilgrimage.

---

2. As we were writing this, Ireland's most respected newspaper even suggested that *Domhnach Chrom Dubh* should replace 17th March (the present St Patrick's Day) as Ireland's national day. St Patrick's Day 1979 was celebrated in a blizzard; we watched the Dublin parade and felt desperately sorry for the drenched and frozen majorettes, clad in little more than braided tunics and brave smiles. Two days later *The Irish Times* in a first leader headed "Why March 17?", asked: "Would it not be better for all if the national holiday were celebrated when our weather is more bland? There is one day which is, if not historically, at least in the legendary sense, apposite and from the weather point of view more acceptable. That is the last Sunday in July, Garland Sunday or *Domhnach Chrom Dubh*." Citing Máire MacNeill's *The*

The Sacrifice of Crom himself seems to have been enacted in very ancient times by the sacrifice of human substitutes at a phallic stone surrounded by twelve other stones (the sacrificial hero-king's traditional number of companions). The eleventh-century *Book of Leinster* says, with Christian distaste:

"In a rank stand
Twelve idols of stone;
Bitterly to enchant the people
The figure of the Cromm was of gold."

This was at Magh Sléacht ('The Plain of Adoration'), generally held to be around Killycluggin in County Cavan, where there is a stone circle and the shattered remains of a phallic stone carved with Iron Age decorations—in keeping with the tradition that St Patrick overthrew the Crom stone.

Later the sacrifice seems to have been that of a bull, of which there are many hints, though only one which can be specifically linked with Crom Dubh. That is from the north shore of Galway Bay. "It tells of the tradition that a beef-animal was skinned and roasted to ashes in honour of Crom Dubh on his festival day, and that this had to be done by every householder." (MacNeill, *ibid.*, p. 407.) Many legends speak of the death and resuscitation of a sacred bull (*ibid.*, p. 410). And, accepting that Croagh Patrick must have been a sacrificial mountain long before St Patrick took it over, we cannot help wondering if there is significance in the fact that Westport, the town that commands its approaches, has for its Gaelic name Cathair na Mart, 'City of the Beeves'.

But underlying all the legends we have mentioned so far is an older fertility theme, which shines through many of the still-remembered festival customs. Balor, Bres and Crom Dubh are all forms of the Elder God, to whom belongs the *power* to produce. Along comes his son/other-self, the bright Young God, Horus to his Osiris—the many-gifted Lugh, who wrests

---

Festival of Lughnasa to support its argument, it ended: "If any interest, therefore, wants to sponsor another date, and a valid one, for remembering our Saint, the folklore files give a ready answer." Ireland's gift for pagan-Christian continuity is clearly indestructible; we are tempted to wonder whether, in this epoch of religious change, it will work both ways!

from him the *fruits* of that power. Even the colourful St Patrick legends echo this victory. "Saint Patrick must be a latecomer to the mythological legends and must have displaced a former actor. If we restore Lugh to the role taken by Saint Patrick, the legends at once acquire new meaning." (MacNeill, *ibid.*, p. 409.)

In the legends of this fertility-victory (and also doubtless, as Máire MacNeill points out, at one time in the enacted Lughnasadh ritual), Crom Dubh is often buried in the ground up to the neck for three days and then released once the harvest-fruits have been guaranteed.

A sign of the success of the rite is given by—of all things—the humble bilberry (whortle-berry, blaeberry). *Domhnach Chrom Dubh* has other names (including Garland Sunday and Garlic Sunday), and one of them is Fraughan Sunday, from the Gaelic *fraochán* or *fraochóg* for bilberry. On that day still, young people go picking bilberries, with various traditional jollifications, though the custom seems unfortunately to be waning. The forms of the tradition make it quite clear that the bilberries were regarded as a reciprocal gift from the God, a sign that the Lughnasadh ritual had succeeded; their plentifulness or otherwise was taken as a forecast of the size of the harvest. The fact that the two rituals are complementary is still underlined in our locality by the fact that, while adults climb Croagh Patrick on *Domhnach Chrom Dubh*, children are climbing the mountains of the Curraun peninsula, just across the bay, to pick bilberries.

Another Fraughan Sunday site is Carrigroe near Ferns in County Wexford, a 771-foot mountain on the flank of which our first Irish home stood. Within living memory, large crowds used to gather there for the picking, and flowers would be placed on the Giant's Bed, a shelf in the rock which forms the summit. (Our Plate 11 was photographed on that rock.) The fertility association is specific in the joke made to us by more than one neighbour—that half the population of Ferns was conceived on the Giant's Bed; though doubtless that particular ritual has become private rather than communal!

(Incidentally, folk-memories of the magical significance of that little mountain are enshrined in an unwritten local saying, passed to us independently by at least two neighbours, both of whom made it clear they were commenting on our presence there as witches: "As long as Carrigroe stands, there will be people who know." We certainly found it magically super-charged.)

Throughout Britain and Ireland, Christianity notwithstanding, the May Eve greenwood lovemaking which so shocked the Puritans found its cheerful echo not only among the bilberries but in the Lammas (Lughnasadh) cornfields; on which theme, if you like songs at your Sabbats, Robert Burns's *It was upon a Lammas Night*—

> "Corn rigs, an' barley rigs,
> An' corn rigs are bonnie;
> I'll ne'er forget that happy night,
> Amang the rigs wi' Annie"

—is both appropriate and delightful.

The Three Machas—the Triple Goddess in her battle aspect—appear as the triune patroness of the Lughnasadh festival, bringing us back to the sacrificial theme. Another hint is that it was at Lammas that King William Rufus fell to Sir Walter Tyrell's 'accidental' arrow in the New Forest in 1100—a death which, as Margaret Murray and others have persuasively argued, was in fact his willing ritual sacrifice at the end of his term as Divine King and was so understood and honoured by his people. (The nursery rhyme 'Who Killed Cock Robin?' is said to commemorate this event.)

But what of the sacrificial mating theme *as a single concept*, instead of as two separate ones of sacrifice and sexuality? Has this vanished altogether in Irish tradition?

Not quite. In the first place, that tradition as it has reached us is mainly a God-and-Hero one, though with the Goddess hovering powerfully in the background; and it has reached us largely through mediaeval Christian monks who wrote down a body of *oral* legend (albeit surprisingly sympathetically)—scribes whose conditioning perhaps made it difficult for them to recognize Goddess clues. But the clues are there—particularly in the recurrent theme of the rivalry of two heroes (gods) over a heroine (goddess). This theme is not confined to the Irish Celts; it appears, for example, in the legend of Jack the Tinkard, who can be regarded as a Cornish Lugh. And significantly—as with the Oak King and Holly King, these heroes are often alternately successful.

And what is Crom Dubh's three-day burial up to the neck in Mother Earth, and his release when her fertility is assured, but a sacrificial mating and rebirth?

So, in our own Lughnasadh ritual, we have kept to that theme. When our coven first tried out the Love-Chase enactment of the Sacrificial Mating, at Bealtaine 1977, we found it very successful; it portrayed the theme vividly but without grimness. We saw no reason why it should not be repeated, with modifications appropriate to the harvest season, at Lughnasadh; and that is what we have done.

Because the High Priestess at Lughnasadh invokes the Goddess into herself and delays this invocation until after the 'death' of the Holly King, we felt it more suitable in the Opening Ritual to have the High Priest deliver the Charge for her; he *quotes* the Goddess, instead of the High Priestess speaking *as* the Goddess.

Normally, we like to give an active role in the ritual to as many people as possible; but it will be noticed that in this Lughnasadh rite, the men (apart from the High Priest) have practically nothing to do between the Love Chase and the final ring dance. This is in keeping with the tradition surrounding the death of the Corn King; in many places it was a mystery between the women of the tribe and their solitary sacred victim, which no other man was allowed to witness. In our Sabbat, the men can always get their own back during the party-stage forfeits!

The High Priest's declamation "*I am a battle-waging spear . . .*" is again from the Song of Amergin—this time according to Graves's allocation for the second half of the year.

The Preparation

A small loaf is placed on the altar; most suitable is a soft roll or 'bap'.

A green scarf or piece of gauze at least a yard square is laid by the altar.

If cassette music is used, the High Priestess may wish to have one piece of music for the main ritual, plus another of an insistent—even primitive—rhythm for her Corn Dance since it, unlike the Midsummer Dance, is not accompanied by chanting.

The High Priest should have a crown of holly combined with ears of a grain crop. The women many wear grain-crop chaplets, perhaps interwoven with red poppies. Grain, poppies and bilberries, if available, are particularly suitable for the altar, with other seasonal flowers.

The cauldron, decorated with stems of grain, is by the East candle, the quarter of rebirth.

The Ritual

In the opening ritual, Drawing Down the Moon is omitted. The High Priest gives the High Priestess the Fivefold Kiss and then immediately himself delivers the Charge, substituting "she, her, hers" for "I, me, my, mine".

After the Witches' Rune, the coven spread themselves around the Circle and start a soft, rhythmic clapping.

The High Priest picks up the green scarf, gathers it lengthwise like a rope and holds it with one end in each hand. He starts to move towards the High Priestess, making as though to throw the scarf over her shoulders and pull her to him; but she backs away from him, tantalizingly.

While the coven continue their rhythmic clapping, the High Priestess continues to elude the pursuing High Priest. She beckons to him and teases him but always steps back before he can capture her with the scarf. She weaves in and out of the coven, and the other women step in the High Priest's way to help her elude him.

After a while, say after two or three 'laps' of the Circle, the High Priestess allows the High Priest to capture her by throwing the scarf over her head to behind her shoulders and pulling her to him. They kiss and separate, and the High Priest hands the scarf to another man.

The other man then pursues *his* partner, who eludes him, beckons to him and teases him in exactly the same way; the clapping goes on all the time. (See Plate 12.) After a while she, too, allows herself to be captured and kissed.

The man then hands the scarf to another man, and the pursuit-game continues until every couple in the room has taken part.

The last man hands the scarf back to the High Priest.

Once again the High Priest pursues the High Priestess; but this time the pace is much slower, almost stately, and her eluding and beckoning more solemn, as though she is tempting him into danger; and this time the others do not intervene. The pursuit continues until the High Priestess places herself facing the altar and two or three paces from it; the High Priest halts with his back to the altar and captures her with the scarf.

They embrace solemnly but wholeheartedly; but after a few seconds of the kiss, the High Priest lets the scarf fall from his hands, and the High Priestess releases him and takes a step backwards.

The High Priest drops to his knees, sits back on his heels and lowers his head, chin on chest.

The High Priestess spreads her arms, signalling for the clapping to stop. She then calls forward two women by name and places them one each side of the High Priest, facing inwards, so that the three of them tower over him. The High Priestess picks up the scarf, and the three of them spread it between them over the High Priest. They lower it slowly and then release it, so that it covers his head like a shroud.

The coven now spread themselves around the perimeter of the Circle, facing inwards.

The High Priestess may then, if she wishes, change the music-cassette to her chosen dance theme or signal someone else to do so.

She then picks up the small loaf from the altar and holds it for a moment just above the bowed head of the High Priest. She then goes to the middle of the Circle, holds the loaf up high in the direction of the altar and invokes:

"O Mighty Mother of us all, bringer of all fruitfulness, give us fruit and grain, flocks and herds, and children to the tribe, that we may be mighty. By the rose of thy love,[3] *do thou descend upon the body of thy servant and priestess here."*

---

3. The Book of Shadows says "by thy rosy love". Doreen Valiente queried this "rather meaningless phrase" with Gardner at the time, suggesting it might be a corruption of "by thy rose of love" or "by the rose of thy love"—the rose being a symbol of the Goddess as well as Britain's national flower. We have followed the second of her suggestions.

After a moment's pause, and gently at first, she starts her
Corn Dance, all the time carrying the loaf as a sacred and
magical object. [1] (See Plate 13.)

She finishes her dance by standing facing the High Priest
(who is still motionless and 'dead') with the loaf in her two
hands, and saying:

"Gather round, O Children of the Harvest!"

The rest of the coven gather round the High Priestess and the
kneeling High Priest. (If the High Priestess and the Maiden do
not know their words by heart, the Maiden may bring the script
and one altar candle and stand beside the High Priestess where
they both can read it, since the High Priestess's hands are both
occupied.)

The High Priestess says:

*"Behold, the Holly King is dead—he who is also the Corn King.
He has embraced the Great Mother, and died of his love; so has it
been, year by year, since time began. But if the Holly King is
dead—he who is the God of the Waning Year—all is dead; all that
sleeps in my womb of Earth would sleep forever. What shall we do,
therefore, that the Holly King may live again?"*

The Maiden says:

*"Give us to eat the bread of Life. Then shall sleep lead on to
rebirth."*

The High Priestess says:

"So mote it be."

(The Maiden may now replace the script and the altar candle
and return to her place beside the High Priestess.)

The High Priestess breaks small pieces from the loaf and
gives one piece to each witch, who eats it. She does not yet eat a
piece herself but keeps enough in her hands for at least three
more portions.

She summons the original two women to stand on either side
of the High Priest. When they are in position, she gestures to
them to lift the scarf from the High Priest's head; they do so and
lay it on the floor.

---

4. Like the Midsummer Dance, the Corn Dance may be delegated by the
High Priestess to another woman if she wishes. In this case, she will hand the
loaf to the dancer after the invocation and receive it back after the dance,
before she takes her place facing the High Priest.

The High Priestess says:
"Come back to us, Holly King, that the land may be fruitful."
The High Priest rises, and says:

> *"I am a battle-waging spear;*
> *I am a salmon in the pool;*
> *I am a hill of poetry;*
> *I am a ruthless boar;*
> *I am a threatening noise of the sea;*
> *I am a wave of the sea;*
> *Who but I knows the secrets of the unhewn dolmen?"*

The High Priestess then gives him a piece of the loaf and takes a piece herself; they both eat, and she replaces the last of the loaf on the altar. High Priestess and High Priest then lead a ring dance, building up the pace so that it becomes more and more joyous, until the High Priestess cries "Down!" and everybody sits.

The Great Rite is then enacted.

The remaining portion of the loaf, after the Circle has been banished, becomes part of the Earth-offering along with the last of the wine and cakes.

IX   Autumn Equinox, 21st September

The two Equinoxes are, as we have pointed out, times of equilibrium. Day and night are matched, and the tide of the year flows steadily. But while the Spring Equinox manifests the equilibrium of an athlete poised for action, the Autumn Equinox's theme is that of rest after labour. The Sun is about to enter the sign of Libra, the Balance. In the Stations of the Goddess, the Spring Equinox represents Initiation; the Autumn Equinox, Repose. The harvest has been gathered in, both grain and fruit, yet the Sun—though mellower and less fierce than he was—is still with us. With symbolic aptness, there is still a week to go before Michaelmas, the festival of Michael/Lucifer, Archangel of Fire and Light, at which we must begin to say *au revoir* to his splendour.

Doreen Valiente (*An ABC of Witchcraft*, p. 166) remarks that the most frequent spectral appearances of certain recurrent hauntings are March and September, "the months of the Equinoxes—periods well known to occultists as being times of psychic stress". That would seem to contradict the idea of the Equinoxes being times of balance; yet the paradox is only an apparent one. Times of balance, of suspended activity, are by their nature the times when the veil between the seen and the unseen is thin. They are also the seasons when human beings 'change gear' to a different phase, and therefore times of psychological as well as psychic turbulence. That is all the more reason for us to recognize and understand the significance of those natural phases, so that their turbulence exhilarates instead of distressing us.

If we look at the Tree Calendar which Robert Graves has shown to underlie so much of our Western magical and poetic symbolism, we find that the Autumn Equinox comes just before the end of the Vine month and the beginning of the Ivy month. Vine and Ivy are the only two of the month-trees which grow spirally—and the spiral (particularly the double spiral, winding and returning) is a universal symbol of reincarnation. And the bird of the Autumn Equinox is the Swan, another symbol of the immortality of the soul—as is the wild goose, whose domestic variety is the traditional Michaelmas dish.

Incidentally, blackberry is a frequent substitute for the Vine in the symbolism of northern countries. Folk-tradition in many places, particularly in the West of England, insists that black-berries should not be eaten after the end of September (which is also the end of the Vine-month) because they then become the property of the Devil. Might we guess that this means: "Don't try to cling to the incoming spiral once it is over—look onward to the outgoing"?[1]

Lughnasadh marked the actual gathering of the grain harvest, but in its sacrificial aspect; the Autumn Equinox marks the *completion* of the harvest, and thanksgiving for abundance, with the emphasis on the future return of that abundance. This Equinox was the time of the Eleusinian Mysteries, the greatest

---

1. In Ireland, on the other hand, the last day for gathering blackberries is Samhain Eve. After that, the Pooka (see p. 122) "spits on them", hence one of his names—*Púca na sméar*, 'the blackberry sprite'.

mysteries of ancient Greece; and although all the details are not known (initiates kept the secrets well), the rituals of Eleusis certainly based themselves on corn-harvest symbolism. The climax is said to have been the showing to the initiate of a single ear of grain, with the admonition: "In silence is the seed of wisdom gained."

For our own Autumn Sabbat, then, we take the following interrelated themes: the completion of the harvest; a salute to the waning power of the Sun; and an acknowledgement that Sun and harvest, and men and women also, share in the universal rhythm of rebirth and reincarnation. As the Book of Shadows declamation says: "Therefore the Wise Ones weep not, but rejoice."

In the Book of Shadows ritual for this festival, the only substantial items are the High Priestess's declamation "Farewell, O Sun . . ." and the Candle Game, both of which we have retained.

The Preparation

On the altar is a dish containing a single ear of wheat or other cereal crop, covered by a cloth.

The altar and Circle are decorated with pine-cones, grain, acorns, red poppies (symbol of the Corn-Goddess Demeter) and other autumnal flowers, fruit and leaves.

The Ritual

After the Witches' Rune, the coven arrange themselves round the perimeter of the Circle, facing inwards.

The Maiden fetches the covered dish from the altar, places it in the centre of the Circle (leaving it covered) and returns to her place.

The High Priestess says:

"*Now is the time of balance, when Day and Night face each other as equals. Yet at this season the Night is waxing and the Day is waning; for nothing ever remains without change, in the tides of Earth and Sky. Know and remember, that whatsoever rises must also set, and whatsoever sets must also rise. In token of which, let us dance the Dance of Going and Returning!*"

With the High Priestess and High Priest leading, the coven dance slowly widdershins, hand in hand but not closing the ring head-to-tail. Gradually, the High Priestess leads inwards in a spiral, until the coven are close to the centre. When she is ready, the High Priestess halts and instructs everyone to sit in a tight ring about the covered dish, facing inwards.

The High Priestess says:

"*Behold the mystery: in silence is the seed of wisdom gained.*"

She then takes the cloth from the dish, revealing the ear of grain. All contemplate the ear of grain for a while in silence. (See Plate 14.)

When she is ready, the High Priestess rises and goes to the East candle. The High Priest rises and goes to the West candle, and they face each other across the seated coven. The High Priestess declaims:[2]

"Farewell, O Sun, ever-returning Light,
The hidden God, who ever yet remains.
He now departs to the Land of Youth
Through the Gates of Death
To dwell enthroned, the judge of Gods and men,
The hornèd leader of the hosts of air.
Yet, as he stands unseen without the Circle,
So dwelleth he within the secret seed—
The seed of new-reaped grain, the seed of flesh;
Hidden in earth, the marvellous seed of the stars.
In him is Life, and Life is the Light of man,
That which was never born, and never dies.
Therefore the Wise Ones weep not, but rejoice."

The High Priestess raises both hands high in blessing to the High Priest, who responds with the same gesture.

High Priestess and High Priest rejoin the coven (who now stand) and lead them in a slow dance deosil, gradually spiralling outwards towards the perimeter of the Circle. When she judges that the spiral movement has been sufficiently emphasized, the High Priestess closes the ring by taking the hand of the last witch in the chain and speeds up the pace till the coven are

---

2. Written by Doreen Valiente. In Ireland, instead of "*to the Land of Youth*", we say "*to Tír na nÓg*" (pronounced 'teer nuh *noge*') which means literally the same thing but has powerful legendary associations—a Celtic Elysium visualized as a magical island off the West Coast of Ireland, "where happiness can be had for a penny".

circling fast and joyously. After a while she cries "*Down!*" and everybody sits.

The Maiden replaces the dish with the ear of grain on the altar, and the cloth which covered it beside the altar.

The Great Rite is now enacted, followed by the wine and cakes.

After the wine and cakes comes the Candle Game, as described on p. 71 for Imbolg; and that should put everyone in the right frame of mind for the party stage.

X Samhain, 31st October

The eve of 1st November, when the Celtic Winter begins, is the dark counterpart of May Eve which greets the Summer. More than that, 1st November for the Celts was the beginning of the year itself, and the feast of Samhain was their New Year's Eve, the mysterious moment which belonged to neither past nor present, to neither this world nor the Other. Samhain (pronounced 'sow-in', the 'ow' rhyming with 'cow') is Irish Gaelic for the month of November; Samhuin (pronounced 'sav-en', with the 'n' like the 'ni' in 'onion') is Scottish Gaelic for All Hallows, 1st November.

For the old pastoralists, whose herd-raising was backed by only primitive agriculture or none at all, keeping whole herds fed through the winter was simply not possible, so the minimum breeding-stock was kept alive, and the rest were slaughtered and salted—the only way, then, of preserving meat (hence, no doubt, the traditional use in magical ritual of salt as a 'disinfectant' against psychic or spiritual evil). Samhain was the time when this killing and preserving was done; and it is not hard to imagine what a nervously critical occasion it was. Had the right—or enough—breeding-stock been selected? Would the coming winter be long and hard? And if so, would the breeding-stock survive it, or the stored meat feed the tribe through it?

Crops, too, had all to be gathered in by 31st October, and anything still unharvested was abandoned—because of the Pooka (*Púca*), a nocturnal, shape-changing hobgoblin who delighted in tormenting humans, was believed to spend Samhain night destroying or contaminating whatever remained unreaped. The Pooka's favourite disguise seems to have been the shape of an ugly black horse.

Thus to economic uncertainty was added a sense of psychic eeriness, for at the turn of the year—the old dying, the new still unborn—the Veil was very thin. The doors of the *sidh*-mounds were open, and on this night neither human nor fairy needed any magical password to come and go. On this night, too, the spirits of dead friends sought the warmth of the Samhain fire and communion with their living kin. This was *Féile na Marbh* (pronounced '*fay*luh nuh *morv*'), the Feast of the Dead, and also *Féile Moingfhinne* (pronounced '*fay*luh *mong*-innuh'), the Feast of the White-Haired One, the Snow Goddess. It was "a partial return to primordial chaos . . . the dissolution of established order as a prelude to its recreation in a new period of time", as Proinsias mac Cana says in *Celtic Mythology*.

So Samhain was on the one hand a time of propitiation, divination and communion with the dead, and on the other, an uninhibited feast of eating, drinking and the defiant affirmation of life and fertility in the very face of the closing dark.

Propitiation, in the old days when survival was felt to depend on it, was a grim and serious affair. There can be little doubt that at one time it involved human sacrifice—of criminals saved up for the purpose or, at the other end of the scale, of an ageing king; little doubt, either, that these ritual deaths were by fire, for in Celtic (and, come to that, Norse) mythology many kings and heroes die at Samhain, often in a burning house, trapped by the wiles of supernatural women. Drowning may follow the burning, as with the sixth-century Kings of Tara, Muirchertach mac Erca and Diarmait mac Cerbaill.[1]

Later, of course, the propitiatory sacrifice became symbolic, and English children still unwittingly enact this symbolism on Guy Fawkes' Night, which has taken over from the Samhain bonfire. It is interesting that, as the failed assassinator of a king, the burned Guy is in a sense the king's substitute.

Echoes of the Samhain royal sacrifice may also have lingered in that of animal substitutes. Our village Garda (policeman), Tom Chambers, a knowledgeable student of County Mayo

---

1. These two are interesting. In *Lebor Gabála Érenn*, Part V (see Bibliography under MacAlister), we find (in translation from Old Irish): "Now the death of Muirchertach was in this manner; he was drowned in a vat of wine, after being burned, on Samain night on the summit of Cletech over the Boyne; whence St Cairnech said:—

'I am afraid of the woman
about whom many blasts shall play;
for the man who shall be burnt in fire,
on the side of Cletech wine shall drown him'."

The woman was Muirchertach's witch mistress Sín (pronounced 'Sheen', and meaning 'storm') on account of whom St Cairnech cursed him; the men of Ireland sided with the king and Sín against the Bishop. The King felt she was "a goddess of great power", but she said that, although she had great magical power, she was of the race of Adam and Eve. Sín is clearly a priestess of the Dark Goddess, presiding over a communally-approved sacrifice in spite of her personal grief. (The version that she brought about the King's doom in revenge for his slaying of her father seems a later rationalization.) Of her own subsequent death the *Lebor* says: "Sín daughter of Sige of the *sídh*-mounds of Breg died, repeating her names—

'Sighing, Moaning, Blast without reproach,
Rough and Wintry Wind,
Groaning, Weeping, a saying without falsehood—
These are my names on any road.' "

The story of Muirchertach and Sín is told in the Reeses' *Celtic Heritage*, p. 338 onwards, and in Markale's *Women of the Celts*, pp. 167–8.

Diarmait mac Cerbaill, according to the *Lebor*, was killed by Black Aed mac Suibne after a reign of twenty-one years (the sacrificed king's traditional multiple of seven?). The *Lebor* says Aed "stopped, vexed, slew, burnt and swiftly drowned him", which again has all the hallmarks of ritual sacrifice; and Gearóid MacNiocaill says Diarmait "was almost certainly a pagan" (*Ireland Before the Vikings*, p. 26).

history and folklore, tells us that within living memory cockerels' blood was sprinkled at the corners of houses, inside and out, on Martinmas Eve as a protective spell. Now Martinmas is 11th November—which is 1st November *according to the old Julian calendar*, a displacement which often points to the survival of a particularly unofficial custom (see footnote on p. 95). So this may well have been originally a Samhain practice.

The ending of the custom of actual royal sacrifice is perhaps commemorated in the legend of the destruction of Aillen mac Midgna, of the Finnachad *sidhe*, who is said to have burned royal Tara every Samhain until Fionn mac Cumhal finally slew him. (Fionn mac Cumhal is a Robin Hood-type hero, whose legends are remembered all over Ireland. The mountains above our village of Ballycroy are called the Nephin Beg range, which Tom Chambers renders from the Old Irish as 'the little resting-place of Finn'.)

Ireland's bonfire-and-firework night is still Hallowe'en, and some of the unconscious survivals are remarkable. When we lived at Ferns in County Wexford, many of the children who ambushed us at Hallowe'en hoping for apples, nuts or "money for the King, money for the Queen" included one who was masked as 'the Man in Black'. He would challenge us with "I am the Man in Black—do you know me?"—to which we had to reply "I know who you are, but you are the Man in Black." We wonder if he realized that one of the significantly recurrent pieces of evidence in the witchcraft trials of the persecution period is that 'the Man in Black' was the coven's High Priest, whose anonymity must be stubbornly protected.

In Scotland and Wales, individual family Samhain fires used to be lit; they were called *Samhnagan* in Scotland and *Coel Coeth* in Wales and were built for days ahead on the highest ground near to the house. This was still a thriving custom in some districts almost within living memory, though by then it had become (like England's bonfire night) mostly a children's celebration. The habit of Hallowe'en fires survived in the Isle of Man, too.

Frazer, in *The Golden Bough* (pp. 831-3), describes several of these Scottish, Welsh and Manx survivals, and it is very interesting that, both in these and in the corresponding Bealtaine fire customs which he records (pp. 808–14), there are many traces of the choosing of a sacrificial victim by lot—sometimes through distributing pieces of a newly baked cake. In Wales, once the last spark of the Hallowe'en fire was extinguished, everyone would "suddenly take to their heels, shouting at the top of their voices 'The cropped black sow seize the hindmost!'" (Frazer might have added that in Welsh mythology the sow represents the Goddess Cerridwen in her dark aspect.) All these victim-choosing rituals long ago mellowed into a mere romp, but Frazer had no doubt of their original grim purpose. What was once a deadly serious ritual at the great tribal fire had become a party game at the family ones.

Talking of which, at Callander (familiar to British television-viewers of a few years ago as the 'Tannochbrae' of *Dr Finlay's Casebook*) a slightly different method prevailed at the Hallowe'en bonfire. "When the fire had died down," Frazer says, "the ashes were carefully collected in the form of a circle, and a stone was put in, near the circumference, for every person of the several families interested in the bonfire. Next morning, if any of these stones was found to be displaced or injured, the people made sure that the person represented by it was *fey*, or devoted, and that he could not live twelve months from that day." Was this a midway stage between the ancient sacrificial-victim rite and today's Hallowe'en party custom of cheerful divination from the way in which fire-roasted nuts jump?

The divination aspect of Samhain is understandable for two reasons. First, the psychic climate of the season favoured it; and second, anxiety about the coming winter demanded it. Origin-ally the Druids were "surfeited with fresh blood and meat until they became entranced and prophesied", reading the omens for the tribe for the coming year (Cottie Burland, *The Magical Arts*); but in folklore survival the divination became more personal. In particular, young women sought to identify the husband-to-be, by the way roasting nuts jumped (see above) or by conjuring up his image in a mirror. In County Donegal, a girl would wash her nightdress three times in running water and hang it in front of the kitchen fire to dry at midnight on Samhain Eve, leaving the door open; her future husband would be drawn to enter and turn it over. An alternative formula said that the washing water should be brought "from a well which brides and burials pass over". Another widespread method was for a girl to lay her table with a tempting meal, to which the 'fetch' of her future husband would come and, having eaten, be bound to her. (The 'fetch' is of course the projected astral body— implying that at Samhain not only was the veil between matter and spirit very thin but also the astral was less firmly bound to the physical.)

Hallowe'en nuts and apples still have their divinatory aspect in popular tradition; but like the nut-gathering of Bealtaine, their original meaning was a fertility one, for Samhain, too, was a time of deliberate (and tribally purposeful) sexual freedom. This fertility-ritual aspect is, as one might expect, reflected in the legends of gods and heroes. The god Angus mac Óg, and the hero Cu Chulainn, both had Samhain affairs with women who could shape-change into birds; and at Samhain the Dagda (the 'Good God') mated with the Morrigan (the dark aspect of the Goddess) as she bestrode the River Unius, and also with Boann, goddess of the River Boyne.

Samhain, like the other pagan festivals, was so deeply rooted in popular tradition that Christianity had to try to take it over. The aspect of communion with the dead, and with other spirits, was Christianized as All Hallows, moved from its original date of 13th May to 1st November, and extended to the whole Church by Pope Gregory IV in 834. But its pagan overtones remained uncomfortably alive, and in England the Reformation abolished All Hallows. It was not formally restored by the Church of England until 1928, "on the assumption that the old pagan associations of Hallowe'en were at last really dead and forgotten; a supposition that was certainly premature" (Doreen Valiente, *An ABC of Witchcraft*).

As for the feast itself—in the banquet sense, the original food was of course a proportion of the newly slaughtered cattle, roasted in the purifying Samhain fire, and doubtless having the nature of ritually offered 'first fruits'; the fact that the priesthood had first call on it for divinatory purposes, and that what they did not use provided a feast for the tribe, points to this.

In later centuries, ritual food known as 'sowens' was consumed. Robert Burns refers to it in his poem *Hallowe'en*:

"Till butter'd sowens, wi' fragrant lunt,
Set a' their gabs a-steerin' . . ."

—and in his own notes to the poem, says "Sowens, with butter instead of milk to them, is always the Hallowe'en Supper." The *Oxford English Dictionary* defines Sowens as 'an article of diet formerly in common use in Scotland (and in some parts of Ireland), consisting of farinaceous matter extracted from the bran or husks of oats by steeping in water, allowed to ferment slightly and prepared by boiling", and says that it probably derives from *sugh* or *subh*, 'sap'. Maybe—but it is interesting that 'sowen' is nearly enough the pronunciation of 'Samhain'.

In Ireland, 'barm brack', a dark brown loaf or cake made with dried fruit, is as much a feature of Hallowe'en as Christmas pudding is of Christmas and retains the seasonal divinatory function by incorporating tokens which the lucky or unlucky eater finds in his slice. The wrapper of a commercial barm brack in front of us at the moment bears a witch-and-broomstick design and the information: "Contains—ring, marriage in twelve months; pea, poverty; bean, wealth; stick, will beat life partner; rag, old maid or bachelor." The shops are full of them from mid-October. For home-made barm brack, the essential item is the ring. The cake has to be cut and buttered by a married person, out of sight of those who will be eating it.

For any dead friends whose spirits might be visiting, Irish families used to leave some tobacco and a dish of porridge—and some empty chairs—by the fire.

Paul Huson, in his interesting but magically amoral book *Mastering Witchcraft*, says: "The Dumb Supper may be performed in honour of the beloved dead, and wine and bread be ceremonially offered to them, the latter in the shape of a cake made in nine segments similar to the square of Earth." He probably means the Square of Saturn, which has nine segments like a noughts-and-crosses game (and which Huson himself gives on p. 140 of his book.) There are magic squares also for Jupiter (sixteen segments), Mars (twenty-five), Sun (thirty-six), Venus (forty-nine), Mercury (sixty-four) and Moon (eighty-one), but none for Earth. In any case, Saturn would be more seasonally appropriate; he has strong links with both the Holly

King and the Lord of Misrule—in fact the three overlap and merge a good deal.

One thing Samhain has always been, and still is: a lusty and wholehearted feast, a Mischief Night, the start of the reign of that same Lord of Misrule, which traditionally lasts from now till Candlemas—yet with serious undertones. It is not that we surrender to disorder but, as Winter begins, we look 'primordial chaos' in the face so that we may discern in it the seeds of a new order. By challenging it, and even laughing with it, we proclaim our faith that the Goddess and the God cannot, by their very nature, allow it to sweep us away.

How, then, to celebrate Samhain as twentieth-century witches?

One immediate suggestion which has become our habit, and which others may find helpful, is to have *two* celebrations—one the Samhain ritual for the coven itself, and the other the Hallowe'en party for coven, children and friends. Children expect some fun out of Hallowe'en, and so (we have discovered) do friends and neighbours expect something of witches at Hallowe'en. So hold a party and give it to them—pumpkins, masks, fancy-dress, leg-pulls, music, forfeits, local traditions— the lot. And hold your coven Samhain ritual on a separate night.

A general point arises here: how important is it to hold Sabbats on the exact traditional nights? We would say it is preferable, but not vital. The fact must be faced that for Esbats and Sabbats alike, many covens *have* to meet on particular nights—usually at weekends—for reasons of jobs, travel, baby-minding and so on. Even the Charge admits this by saying "*better* it be when the moon is full"—not "it *must* be". And as for Sabbats, most witches feel none the worse for holding them on (say) the nearest Saturday to the true date.

In *Quest* magazine of March 1978, 'Diana Demdike' makes a good point on the subject of celebrating festivals before or after the true date. "It is always better to be late rather than early," she says, "for know it or not, you are working with the powers of magical earth tides, and these begin at the actual solar point in time, so to work before then means you are meeting in the lowest ebb of the previous tide, not very helpful."

At Samhain, to be practical, there is an additional consideration: in many places (including America, Ireland and parts of

Britain) privacy on 31st October cannot be guaranteed. To have your serious Samhain ritual disturbed by children demanding "trick or treat", or "money for the King, money for the Queen", or by neighbours waving lighted pumpkins in your front garden and rightly expecting to be invited in for a drink, is clearly not a good idea. So "better it be" perhaps to displace your Samhain Sabbat by a night or two, and to face Hallowe'en Night itself with the appropriate nuts, apples, small change and bottles ready to hand—or, even better, throw a party. It is not the business of witches to do anything which might seem to discourage, or even to exclude themselves from, such traditional celebrations.

In fact, local tradition should always be respected—all the more so if it is a genuinely living one. That is why, out here in County Mayo, we light our Midsummer bonfire on St John's Eve, 23rd June, when many others dot the landscape far and wide like orange stars in the dusk; we light our Lughnasadh bonfire on *Domhnach Chrom Dubh*, the last Sunday in July, which is still named after one of the old Gods, and to which the many Lughnasadh festival customs that survive in the West of Ireland are attached; and make our Samhain party an outdoor one, weather permitting, for Hallowe'en is family bonfire night throughout Ireland.

But to return to the Samhain ritual itself, which is our concern here. Which of the ancient elements should be included?

Propitiation—no. Propitiation reduces the Gods to a human level of pettiness, in which they have to be bribed and jollied out of their capricious moods of spitefulness and bad temper. It belongs to a very primitive stage of the Old Religion, and survived, we feel, more 'by popular demand' than by priestly wisdom. Modern witches do not *fear* the Gods, the expressions of cosmic power and rhythm; they respect and worship them and work to understand and to put themselves in tune with them. And in rejecting propitiation as a superstition, once understandable but now outgrown, they are not betraying the old wisdom, they are fulfilling it; many of the old priests and priestesses (who had a deeper understanding than some of their more simple followers) would doubtless have smiled approvingly. (Though, in fairness to those 'simple followers', we should add that many rites which to the modern student look like propitiation were in fact nothing of the kind but were sympathetic magic; see *The Golden Bough*, p. 541.)

But the communion with the loved dead, the divination, the feasting, the humour, the affirmation of life—most certainly yes. These are all in accord with the Samhain point in the year's natural, human and psychic rhythms.

On the question of communion with the dead, it should always be remembered that they are *invited*, not summoned. Withdrawal and rest between incarnations is a stage-by-stage process; how long each stage lasts, and what necessary experiences (voluntary or involuntary) are gone through at each stage, is a very individual story, the whole of which can never be known by even the most intimate of the individual's still-incarnated friends. So to force communication with him or her may well be fruitless, or even harmful; and this we feel is the mistake many Spiritualists make, however sincere and genuinely gifted some of their mediums are. So, as Raymond Buckland puts it (*The Tree, The Complete Book of Saxon Witchcraft*, p. 61): "Witches do not 'call Back' the dead. They do not hold *séances*—such belongs to Spiritualism. They do, however, believe that, *if the dead themselves wish it*, they will return at the Sabbat to share in the love and celebration of the occasion."

Any invitation to dead friends, at Samhain or any other time, should be made with this attitude in mind.

As Stewart pointed out in *What Witches Do*: "Of all the eight festivals, this is the one where the Book of Shadows insists most emphatically on the Great Rite. If it is not possible at the time, the Book says the High Priest and High Priestess should celebrate it themselves as soon as convenient, 'in token, or if possible in reality'. The point presumably is that since the Hallowe'en ritual is intimately concerned with death and the dead, it should conclude with a solemn and intense reaffirmation of life."

In the present book, we have assumed that the Great Rite is always possible at the Sabbats, at least in its symbolic form. But we feel that the Book of Shadows' insistence on its particular significance at Samhain is valid, and probably a genuine Craft tradition. So we sought, in our ritual, for a way of giving it that special emphasis—hence the device of the circling coven, which for us achieves the desired effect.

If the 'actual' Great Rite is used, of course, the coven are out of the room, and any means of emphasis must be left to the High Priestess and High Priest enacting it. But the emphasis can still be, so to speak, transmitted to the coven on their return; hence the device of the High Priestess and High Priest blessing the wine and cakes immediately after the return, and the High Priest administering them personally to each woman, and the High Priestess to each man, instead of the usual circulation. We suggest that this personal administering should be carried out also if the Great Rite is symbolic.

The Preparation

The cauldron is placed in the centre of the Circle, with glowing charcoal in a tin lid or other container inside it, and incense to hand. (The usual incense-burner on, or by, the altar can be used at the appropriate moment, but a separate one is better.)

For the High Priestess, make a simple white tabard of chiffon or net (terylene net as sold for curtains will do, though chiffon is prettier). The pattern is easy—two squares or rectangles stitched together along the top and sides, but leaving neck- and arm-slits at the centre of the top, and the tops of the sides. A further refinement can be a third square or rectangle of the same size, with its top edge stitched to the top edge of the other two along the shoulders and the back of the neck-slit; this can hang behind like a cape, or be thrown up and forward over the head and face as a veil. (See diagram and also Plates 7, 11, 16 and 17.)

(Incidentally, we have made a selection of these chiffon tabards, with cape/veils and appropriate braid along the seams and hems, in various colours for various ritual purposes. They can be worn either over robes or over the skyclad body, are cheap and simple to make and are strikingly effective.)

For the Lord of Misrule, make a wand of office, as simple or elaborate as you like. Most elaborate is the traditional court-jester's stick topped by a doll's head and decorated with little bells. Simplest is a plain stick with a rubber balloon (or more traditionally, an inflated pig's bladder) tied to one end. It is laid ready beside the altar.

Circle, altar and cauldron are decorated with seasonal foliage and fruit—among which apples, and if possible nuts on the twig, should feature prominently.

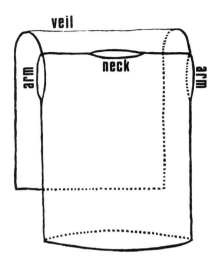

All Sabbats are feasts, but Samhain of course especially so. Food and drink should be ready for the end of the ritual. Nuts should be included, even if you can get only shelled ones at the shop or packets of peanuts from the pub. The tradition of roasting them to read the future from the way they jump (a form of divination best approached in a light-hearted spirit!) is practicable only if you have an open fire in the room.

Personal footnote: we have a tabby cat called Suzie who (alone of our many cats) is our self-appointed familiar. She is very psychic and insists on being present at all rituals; the moment we cast a Circle she bangs on the door to be let in. She behaves very well but has not learned to accept that the feast comes *after* the ritual. So we have to hide the food in a sideboard till the right moment. If you are in the same position, be warned!

The Ritual

The High Priestess wears her white tabard for the opening ritual, with the veil thrown back, if she has one.

After the Witches' Rune, the High Priest and High Priestess

take up their athames. He stands with his back to the altar, she facing him across the cauldron. They then simultaneously draw the Invoking Pentagram of Earth in the air with their athames, towards each other, after which they lay down their athames— he on the altar, she by the cauldron.

The High Priestess scatters incense on the charcoal in the cauldron. When she is satisfied that it is burning, she stands— still facing the High Priest across the cauldron. She summons a male witch to bring one of the altar candles and hold it beside her (so that she can still read her words when, later, she draws her veil over her face). She declaims:[2]

"Dread Lord of Shadows, God of Life, and the Giver of Life—
Yet is the knowledge of thee, the knowledge of Death.
Open wide, I pray thee, the Gates through which all must pass.
Let our dear ones who have gone before
Return this night to make merry with us.
And when our time comes, as it must,
O thou the Comforter, the Consoler, the Giver of Peace and Rest,
We will enter thy realms gladly and unafraid;
For we know that when rested and refreshed among our dear ones
We will be reborn again by thy grace, and the grace of the Great Mother.
Let it be in the same place and the same time as our beloved ones,
And may we meet, and know, and remember,
And love them again.
Descend, we pray thee, in thy servant and priest."

The High Priestess then walks deosil round the cauldron and gives the High Priest the Fivefold Kiss.

She returns to her place, facing the High Priest across the cauldron, and if her tabard has a veil, she now draws it forward over her face. She then calls on each woman witch in turn, by name, to come forward and also give the High Priest the Fivefold Kiss.

When they have all done so, the High Priestess directs the coven to stand around the edge of the Circle, man and woman alternately, with the Maiden next to the West candle. As soon as they are all in place, the High Priestess says:

"Behold, the West is Amenti, the Land of the Dead, to which many of our loved ones have gone for rest and renewal. On this night,

2. Written by Gerald Gardner.

we hold communion with them; and as our Maiden stands in welcome by the Western gate, I call upon all of you, my brothers and sisters of the Craft, to hold the image of these loved ones in your hearts and minds, that our welcome may reach out to them.

"There is mystery within mystery; for the resting-place between life and life is also Caer Arianrhod, the Castle of the Silver Wheel, at the hub of the turning stars beyond the North Wind. Here reigns Arianrhod, the White Lady, whose name means Silver Wheel. To this, in spirit, we call our loved ones. And let the Maiden lead them, moving widdershins to the centre. For the spiral path inwards to Caer Arianrhod leads to night, and rest, and is against the way of the Sun."

The Maiden walks, slowly and with dignity, in a widdershins (anti-clockwise) direction around the Circle, spiralling slowly inwards, taking three or four circuits to reach the centre. During this, the coven maintain absolute silence and concentrate on welcoming their dead friends.

When the Maiden reaches the centre, she faces the High Priestess across the cauldron and halts. The High Priestess holds out her right hand at shoulder level, over the centre of the cauldron, with the palm open and facing to the left. The Maiden places her own right palm flat against that of the High Priestess. The High Priestess says:

"Those you bring with you are truly welcome to our Festival. May they remain with us in peace. And you, O Maiden, return by the spiral path to stand with our brothers and sisters; but deosil—for the way of rebirth, outwards from Caer Arianrhod, is the way of the Sun."

Maiden and High Priestess break their hand-contact, and the Maiden walks slowly and with dignity in a deosil (clockwise) spiral back to her place by the West candle.

The High Priestess waits until the Maiden is in place, and then says:

"Let all approach the walls of the Castle."

The High Priest and the coven move inwards, and everybody (including the High Priestess and the Maiden) sits in a close ring around the cauldron. The High Priestess renews the incense.

Now is the time for communion with dead friends—and for this no set ritual can be laid down, because all covens differ in their approach. Some prefer to sit quietly round the cauldron, gazing into the incense-smoke, talking of what they see and feel. Others prefer to pass round a scrying-mirror or a crystal ball. Other covens may have a talented medium and may use her or him as a channel. Whatever the method, the High Priestess directs it.

When she feels that this part of the Sabbat has fulfilled its purpose, the High Priestess unveils her face and orders the cauldron to be carried and placed beside the East candle, the quarter of rebirth. (It should be put *beside* the candle, not in front of it, to leave room for what follows.)

The High Priest now takes over the explanation. He tells the coven, informally but seriously, that, since Samhain is a festival of the dead, it must include a strong reaffirmation of life—both on behalf of the coven itself and on behalf of the dead friends who are moving towards reincarnation. He and the High Priestess will now, therefore, enact the Great Rite, as is the custom at every Sabbat; but since this is a special occasion, there will be slight differences to emphasize it. He explains these differences, according to the form the Great Rite is going to take.

If the Great Rite is symbolic, the chalice and athame will be placed on the floor, not carried; and the Maiden and the rest of the coven will walk slowly deosil round the perimeter of the Circle during the whole of the Rite. When it is finished, High Priest and High Priestess will first give each other the wine in the usual way; but the High Priest will then personally give the wine to each woman, after which the High Priestess will personally give it to each man. They will then consecrate the cakes and give them out personally in the same way. The purpose of this (the High Priest explains) is to pass on the life-power raised by the Great Rite directly to each member of the coven.

If the Great Rite is 'actual', once the Maiden and coven have returned to the room, High Priest and High Priestess will consecrate the wine and cakes and administer them personally in the same manner.

Explanations over, the Great Rite is enacted.

Afterwards, and before the feast, only one thing remains to be done. The High Priestess fetches the Lord of Misrule's wand of office and presents it to a chosen man witch (preferably one with a sense of humour). She tells him that he is now the Lord of Misrule and for the rest of the Sabbat is privileged to disrupt the proceedings as he sees fit and to 'take the mickey' out of everyone, including herself and the High Priest.

The rest of the programme is given over to the feasting and the games. And if you, like us, are in the habit of putting out a little offering of food and drink afterwards for the *sidhe* or their local equivalent—on this night of all nights, make sure it is particularly tasty and generous!

XI   Yule, 22nd December

At the Winter Solstice, the two God-themes of the year's cycle coincide—even more dramatically than they do at the Summer Solstice. Yule (which, according to the Venerable Bede, comes from the Norse *Iul* meaning 'wheel') marks the death and rebirth of the Sun-God; it also marks the vanquishing of the Holly King, God of the Waning Year, by the Oak King, God of the Waxing Year. The Goddess, who was Death-in-Life at Midsummer, now shows her Life-in-Death aspect; for although at this season she is the "leprous-white lady", Queen of the cold darkness, yet this is her moment for giving birth to the Child of Promise, the Son-Lover who will re-fertilize her and bring back light and warmth to her kingdom.

The Christmas Nativity story is the Christian version of the theme of the Sun's rebirth, for Christ is the Sun-God of the

Piscean Age. The birthday of Jesus is undated in the Gospels, and it was not till AD 273 that the Church took the symbolically sensible step of fixing it officially at midwinter, to bring him in line with the other Sun-Gods (such as the Persian Mithras, also born at the Winter Solstice). As St Chrysostom, Archbishop of Constantinople a century later, explained with commendable frankness, the Nativity of "the Sun of Righteousness" had been so fixed in order that "while the heathen were busied with their profane rites, the Christians might perform their holy ones without disturbance".

"Profane" or "holy" depended on your viewpoint, because basically both were celebrating the same thing—the turning of the year's tide from darkness towards light. St Augustine acknowledged the festival's solar meaning when he urged Christians to celebrate it for him who made the Sun, rather than for the Sun itself.

Mary at Bethlehem is again the Goddess as Life-in-Death. Jerome, the greatest scholar of the Christian Fathers, who lived in Bethlehem from 386 till his death in 420, tells us that there was also a grove of Adonis (Tammuz) there. Now Tammuz, beloved of the Goddess Ishtar, was the supreme model in that part of the world of the Dying and Resurrected God. He was (like most of his type) a vegetation- or corn-god; and Christ absorbed this aspect of the type as well as the solar one, as the Sacrament of the Bread suggests. So as Frazer points out (*The Golden Bough*, p. 455), it is significant that the name Bethlehem means 'the House of Bread'.

The resonance between the corn-cycle and the Sun-cycle is reflected in many customs: for example, the Scottish tradition of keeping the Corn Maiden (the last handful reaped at the harvest) till Yule and then distributing it among the cattle to make them thrive all year; or, in the other direction, the German tradition of scattering the ashes of the Yule Log over the fields, or of keeping its charred remains to bind in the last sheaf of the following harvest.[1] (Here again we meet with the

---

1. Magical transference of fertility from one season to another by a charged physical object—particularly by grain or its products, or by the by-products of fire—is a universal custom. Speaking of the temple of Aphrodite and Eros on the northern slope of the Akropolis, where 'Aphrodite of the Gardens' dwelt,

magical properties of everything about the Sabbat fire, including its ashes; for the Yule Log is, in essence, the Sabbat bonfire driven indoors by the cold of winter.)

But to return to Mary. It was hardly surprising that, for Christianity to remain a viable religion, the Queen of Heaven had to be re-admitted to something like her true status, with a mythology and a popular devotion far outstripping (sometimes even conflicting with) the Biblical data on Mary. She had to be given that status, because she answered what Geoffrey Ashe calls "a Goddess-shaped yearning"—a yearning which four centuries of utterly male-chauvinist Christianity, on both the divine and the human level, had made unbearable. (It should be emphasized that the Church's male chauvinism was *not* inaugurated by Jesus, who treated women as fully human beings, but by the pathologically misogynist and sex-hating St Paul.)

Mary's virtual deification came with startling suddenness, initiated by the Council of Ephesus in 431 "amid great popular rejoicing, due, doubtless, to the hold which the cult of the virgin Artemis still had on the city" (*Encyclopaedia Britannica*, 'Ephesus' entry). Significantly, it coincided closely with the determined suppression of Isis-worship, which had spread throughout the known world. From then on, the theologians strove to discipline Mary, allowing her *hyperdulia* ('super-veneration', a stepped-up version, unique to her, of the *dulia*, veneration, accorded to the saints) but not *latria* (the adoration which was the monopoly of the male God). They managed to create, over the centuries, an official synthesis of the Queen of Heaven, by which they achieved the remarkable double feat of desexualizing the Goddess and dehumanizing Mary. But they could not muffle her power; it is to her that the ordinary worshipper (knowing and caring nothing about the distinction between *hyperdulia* and *latria*) turns, "now and at the hour of our death".

Geoffrey Grigson tells us: "It was to this temple that two girls, two children, paid a ritual visit every spring, bringing with them, from Athene's temple on the summit, loaves shaped like phalluses and snakes. In Aphrodite's temple the loaves acquired the power of fecundity. In autumn they were taken back to the Akropolis, and crumbled into the seed grain, to ensure a good yield after the next sowing." (*The Goddess of Love*, p. 162.)

Protestantism went to the other extreme and in varying degrees tried once again to banish the Goddess altogether. All it achieved was the loss of magic, which Catholicism, in however distorted and crippling a form, retained; for the Goddess cannot be banished.

(For a fuller understanding of the Marian phenomenon, see Ashe's *The Virgin* and Marina Warner's *Alone of All Her Sex*.)

The Goddess at Yule also presides over the other God-theme—that of the Oak King and Holly King, which survived, too, in popular Christmas tradition, however much official theology ignored it. In the Yuletide mumming plays, shining St George slew the dark 'Turkish knight' and then immediately cried out that he had slain his brother. "Darkness and light, winter and summer, are complementary to each other. So on comes the mysterious 'Doctor', with his magical bottle, who revives the slain man, and all ends with music and rejoicing. There are many local variations of this play, but the action is substantially the same throughout." (Doreen Valiente, *An ABC of Witchcraft*, pp. 358–60.) Yuletide mumming still survives locally—for example in Drumquin, County Tyrone, where exotically masked and costumed young farmers go from house to house enacting the age-old theme with words and actions handed down from their ancestors; Radio Telefís Éireann made an excellent film of it as their entry for the 1978 *Golden Harp Festival*.

All too often, of course, the harmonious balance of the dark and light twins, of necessary waxing and waning, has been distorted into a concept of Good-versus-Evil. At Dewsbury in Yorkshire, for nearly seven centuries, church bells have tolled 'the Devil's Knell' or 'the Old Lad's Passing' for the last hour of Christmas Eve, warning the Prince of Evil that the Prince of Peace is coming to destroy him. Then, from midnight on, they peal out a welcome to the Birth. A worthy custom, on the face of it—but in fact it enshrines a sad degradation of the Holly King.

Oddly enough, the popular name 'Old Nick' for the Devil reflects the same demotion. Nik was a name for Woden, who is very much a Holly King figure—as is Santa Claus, otherwise St Nicholas (who in early folklore rode not reindeer but a white horse through the sky—like Woden). So Nik, God of the Waning Year, has been Christianized in two forms: as Satan and as the jolliest of the saints. The Abbot's Bromley Horn Dance (now a September, but once a Yule rite) is based on the parish church of St Nicholas, which suggests a direct continuity from the days when the patron of the locality was not Nicholas but Nik. (On Nik and St Nicholas, see Doreen Valiente's *ABC of Witchcraft*, pp. 258–9.)

Incidentally, in Italy Santa Claus's place is taken by a witch, and a lady witch at that. She is called Befana (Epiphany), and she flies around on Twelfth Night on her broomstick, bringing gifts for children down the chimneys.

An extraordinarily persistent version of the Holly King/Oak King theme at the Winter Solstice is the ritual hunting and killing of the wren—a folklore tradition found as far apart in time and space as ancient Greece and Rome and today's British Isles. The wren, 'little king' of the Waning Year, is killed by his Waxing Year counterpart, the robin redbreast, who finds him hiding in an ivy bush (or sometimes in Ireland in a holly bush, as befits the Holly King). The robin's tree is the birch, which follows the Winter Solstice in the Celtic tree-calendar. In the acted-out ritual, men hunted and killed the wren with birchrods.

In Ireland, the 'Wren Boys'' day is St Stephen's Day, 26th December. In some places (the fishing village of Kilbaha in County Clare on the Shannon estuary, for example), the Wren Boys are groups of adult musicians, singers and dancers in colourful costumes, who go from house to house bearing the tiny effigy of a wren on a bunch of holly. In County Mayo the Wren Boys (and girls) are parties of children, also bearing holly bunches, who knock on our doors and recite their jingle to us:

> "The wren, the wren, the king of the birds,
> On Stephen's Day was caught in the furze;
> Up with the kettle and down with the pan,
> And give us some money to bury the wren."

It used to be 'a penny', but inflation has outstripped tradition. All holly decorations in Ireland must be cleared out of the house after Christmas; it is considered unlucky to let these Waning Year symbols linger.

The apparent absence of a corresponding Midsummer tradition, where one might expect a hunting of the robin, is puzzling.

But there may be a trace of it in the curious Irish belief about a Kinkisha (*Cincíseach*), a child born at Pentecost (*Cincís*), that such a person is doomed either to kill or to be killed—unless the 'cure' is applied. This 'cure' is to catch a bird and squeeze it to death inside the child's hand (while reciting three Hail Marys). In some places at least, the bird has to be a robin, and we feel this is probably the original tradition, for Pentecost is a movable feast, falling anywhere from 10th May to 13th June—i.e., towards the end of the Oak King's reign. It may be that long ago a baby born at this season was in danger of becoming a substitute sacrifice for the Oak King, and what better escape than to find a replacement in the shape of his own bird-substitute, the robin redbreast? And the 'kill or be killed' danger may be a memory of the Oak King's destiny of killing at Midwinter and being killed at Midsummer.[2]

The Waxing Year robin brings us to Robin Hood, cropping up in yet another seasonal festival. "In Cornwall," Robert Graves tells us, " 'Robin' means phallus. 'Robin Hood' is a country name for red campion ('campion' means 'champion'), perhaps because its cloven petal suggests a ram's hoof, and because 'Red Champion' was a title of the Witch-god. . . . 'Hood' (or Hod or Hud) meant 'log'—the log put at the back of the fire—and it was in this log, cut from the sacred oak, that Robin had once been believed to reside—hence 'Robin Hood's steed', the wood-louse which ran out when the Yule log was burned. In the popular superstition Robin himself escaped up the chimney in the form of a robin and, when Yule ended, went out as Belin against his rival Bran, or Saturn—who had been 'Lord of Misrule' at the Yule-tide revels. Bran hid from pursuit in the ivy-bush disguised as a Gold Crest Wren; but Robin always caught and hanged him." (*The White Goddess*, p. 397.)

Mention of the Celtic tree-calendar (and of Graves's *White*

---

2. Substitute sacrifice is by no means dead in Ireland. On a County Mayo headland frequently lashed by storms, a few miles from our home, we have seen a celluloid doll nailed to a post at the high-tide mark. It was naked except for a patch of green paint where the nail penetrated. Our local-tradition expert, Tom Chambers, asked questions for us; as we suspected, it turned out to be a propitiatory sacrifice to the sea and is known as a 'Sea Doll' (*bábóg mhara*).

Goddess, its most detailed modern analysis) brings us back to the Goddess and the Sun-God aspect. As will be seen in our diagram on page 26, Graves's "Five Stations of the Goddess" are distributed round the year, but two of them (Death and Birth) are together on consecutive days at the Winter Solstice, 22nd and 23rd December. The latter is the 'extra day' which does not belong in any of the thirteen tree-months. Before it comes Ruis, the elder-tree month, and after it comes Beth, the birch-tree month. The pattern, whose symbolism will repay study (though preferably in the context of the whole year's calendar) is as follows, around the Winter Solstice:

25th November—22nd December: Ruis, the elder-tree; a tree of doom and of the dark aspect of the Goddess, with white flowers and dark fruit ("Elder is the Lady's tree—burn it not, or cursed you'll be"). Bird, the rook *(rócnat)*; the rook, raven or crow is the prophetic bird of Bran, the Holly-King deity, who is also linked with the wren in Ireland, while in Devonshire the wren is 'the cuddy vran' or 'Bran's sparrow'. Colour, blood-red *(ruadh)*. Line from the Song of Amergin: "I am a wave of the sea" (for weight).

22nd December. Death Station of the Goddess: Tree, the yew *(idho)*, and palm. Metal, lead. Bird, eagle *(illait)*. Colour, very white *(irfind)*.

23rd December The Extra Day; *Birth Station of the Goddess*: Tree, silver fir *(ailm)*, the original Christmas Tree; also mistletoe. Metal, silver. Bird, lapwing *(aidhircleóg)*, the piebald trickster. Colour, piebald *(alad)*. Amergin asks: "Who but I knows the secrets of the unhewn dolmen?"

24th December–20th January: Beth, the birch-tree; a tree of inception and the driving-out of evil spirits. Bird, pheasant *(besan)*. Colour, white *(bán)*. Amergin proclaims: "I am a stag of seven tines" (for strength).

The Winter Solstice rebirth, and the Goddess's part in it, were portrayed in ancient Egypt by a ritual in which Isis circled the shrine of Osiris seven times, to represent her mourning for him and her wanderings in search of the scattered parts of his body. The text of her dirge for Osiris, in which her sister Nephthys (who is in a sense her own dark aspect) joined her, can be found in two somewhat different versions in *The Golden Bough*, p. 482, and Esther Harding's *Woman's Mysteries*, pp.

188–9. Typhon or Set, the brother/enemy who killed him, was driven away by the shaking of Isis's sistrum, to bring about Osiris's rebirth. Isis herself was represented by the image of a cow with the sun-disc between its horns. For the festival, people decorated the outsides of their houses with oil-lamps which burned all night. At midnight, the priests emerged from an inner shrine crying "The Virgin has brought forth! The light is waxing!" and showing the image of a baby to the worshippers. The final entombment of the dead Osiris was on 21st December, after his long mummification ritual (which began, interestingly enough, on 3rd November—virtually at Samhain); on 23rd December his sister/wife Isis gave birth to his son/other-self Horus. Osiris and Horus represent at the same time the solar and the vegetational God-aspects; Horus is both the reborn Sun (the Greeks identified him with Apollo) and 'Lord of the Crops'. Another name of Horus, 'Bull of Thy Mother', reminds us that the God-child of the Goddess is, at another point in the cycle, her lover and impregnator, father in due course to his own reborn self.

The lamps burning all night on the eve of Midwinter survive, in Ireland and elsewhere, as the single candle burning in the window on Christmas Eve, lit by the youngest in the house—a symbol of microcosmic welcome to the Macrocosm, not unlike the extra place laid at a Jewish family's Pesach table (at which table, incidentally, the youngest son, with his question "Father, why is tonight different from all other nights?", also has a traditional part to play).

The owner of our village pub offers her own microcosmic welcome, following a tradition which she tells us was once widespread among Irish innkeepers. She cleans out a stable stall, spreads fresh straw and leaves there some food, a bottle of wine and a baby's bottle of milk—so that there *shall* be 'room at the inn'. She is shy to talk about it but sorry the custom seems to be dying.

A friend who has lived with the Eskimos in Greenland, where Christianity has bulldozed a formerly well-integrated balance of belief and way of life, tells us how Winter Solstice rituals have died without being meaningfully replaced. The Eskimos can hardly be said to celebrate Christmas at all, in comparison with the festival as it is known in the 'older' Christian countries; yet the traditional solstice rites (which apparently were memorable occasions) are no longer observed because they depend on exact reckoning of the solstice by stellar observation—a skill which the present generation no longer possesses. So much for the blessings of technological civilization!

In Athens, the Winter Solstice ritual was the Lenaea, the Festival of the Wild Women. Here, the death and rebirth of the harvest-god Dionysos was enacted. In the dim past it had been a god-sacrifice ritual, and the nine Wild Women had torn his human representative to pieces and eaten him. But by classical times the Titans had become the sacrificers, the victim had been replaced by a goat-kid, and the nine Wild Women had become mourners and witnesses of the birth. (See *The White Goddess*, p. 399.) The Wild Women also appear in northern legend; as the Waelcyrges (Valkyries) they rode with Woden on his Wild Hunt.

In the Book of Shadows Yule ritual, only the rebirth of the Sun-God is featured, with the High Priest calling upon the Goddess to "bring to us the Child of Promise". The Holly King/Oak King theme is ignored—a strange omission in view of its persistence in the folklore of the season.

We have combined the two themes in our ritual, choosing the Oak King and Holly King by lot, as at Midsummer, immediately after the opening ritual—but postponing the 'slaying' of the Holly King until after the death and rebirth of the Sun.

A problem arises over the Oak King's crown; while at Midsummer oak and holly leaves are both available, at Yule oak leaves are not. One answer is to gather oak leaves in advance in the Summer or Autumn, press and lacquer them and make a permanent Oak King's crown for Yuletide use. Another, less fragile perhaps, is to make your permanent crown of acorns when they are in season. Or you can use the winter leaves of the Holm or Evergreen Oak (*Quercus ilex*). Failing all these, make the crown of bare oak twigs but brighten it with Christmas tinsel or other suitable decoration.

At Yule, the Goddess is the 'leprous-white lady', the White-Haired One, Life-in-Death; so we suggest the High Priestess should again wear the white chiffon or net tabard we described for Samhain. A dramatically effective addition, if she possesses one or it can be afforded, is a pure white wig, preferably long. If yours is a skyclad coven, she will take off the tabard before the Great Rite but retain the wig if she is wearing one, because it symbolizes her seasonal aspect.

The High Priestess's lament *"Return, oh, return! . . ."* is a slightly adapted form of Isis's lament for Osiris mentioned above.

If, as is more than likely, you have a Christmas tree in the room, any lights on it should be switched off before the Circle is cast. The High Priest can then switch them on immediately after he lights the cauldron candle.

If there is an open fireplace in the room, a Yule Log can be burned during the Sabbat. It should, of course, be of oak.

The Preparation

The cauldron is placed by the South candle, with an unlit candle inside it, and wreathed with holly, ivy and mistletoe.

Crowns for the Oak King and Holly King are ready beside the altar. A number of straws are laid on the altar—as many as there are men at the Sabbat, except for the High Priest. One of them is longer than the rest, and one shorter. (As at Midsummer, if the High Priestess decides to nominate the two Kings instead of drawing lots, the straws are not needed.)

A blindfold is ready by the altar for the Holly King.

A sistrum for the High Priestess is laid on the altar. The High Priestess shall wear a white tabard and, if she so chooses, a white wig.

If there is a Christmas tree in the room with lights, the lights shall be switched off.

If there is an open fireplace in the room, the fire shall be built up till it is red and glowing, and a Yule Log laid on it just before the Circle is cast.

The Ritual

After the Witches' Rune, the Maiden fetches the straws from the altar and holds them in her hand so that all the ends are protruding separately but nobody can see which are the short and long ones. The High Priestess says:

"Let the men draw lots."

Each man (except the High Priest) draws a straw from the Maiden's hand and shows it to the High Priestess. The High

Priestess points to the man who has drawn the short straw, and says:

"Thou art the Holly King, God of the Waning Year. Maiden, bring his crown!"

The Maiden places the holly-leaf crown on the head of the Holly King.

The High Priestess points to the man who has drawn the long straw, and says:

"Thou are the Oak King, God of the Waxing Year. Maiden, bring his crown!"

The Maiden places the oak-leaf crown on the head of the Oak King.

While the crowning is going on, the High Priest lays himself on the floor in the centre of the Circle, curled up in a foetal position. Everyone pretends not to see him doing this.

When the crowning is over, the Oak King says:

"My brother and I have been crowned and prepared for our rivalry. But where is our Lord the Sun?"

The Maiden replies:

"Our Lord the Sun is dead!"

If the High Priestess's tabard has a veil, she drapes it over her face.

The coven arrange themselves around the perimeter of the Circle.

The High Priestess picks up the sistrum, and the Maiden a candle. They walk together slowly round the High Priest, deosil, seven times. The Maiden holds the candle so that the High Priestess can read her script, and counts quietly *"One,"* *"Two,"* and so on up to *"Seven"* as each circuit is completed. As they go, the High Priestess shakes her sistrum and laments:

> *"Return, oh, return!*
> *God of the Sun, God of the Light, return!*
> *Thine enemies are fled—thou hast no enemies.*
> *O lovely helper, return, return!*
> *Return to thy sister, thy spouse, who loveth thee!*
> *We shall not be put asunder.*
> *O my brother, my consort, return, return!*
> *When I see thee not,*
> *My heart grieveth for thee,*
> *Mine eyes seek for thee,*

> *My feet roam the Earth in search of thee!*
> *Gods and men weep for thee together.*
> *God of the Sun, God of the Light, return!*
> *Return to thy sister, thy spouse, who loveth thee!*
> *Return! Return! Return!"*

When the seven circuits are completed, the High Priestess lays the sistrum on the altar and kneels close to the High Priest, with her hands resting on his body and her back towards the altar. (See Plate 16.)

The coven, except for the Maiden, link hands and move slowly deosil round the High Priestess and High Priest.

The Maiden stands by the altar and declaims:[3]

> *"Queen of the Moon, Queen of the Sun,*
> *Queen of the Heavens, Queen of the Stars,*
> *Queen of the Waters, Queen of the Earth,*
> *Bring to us the Child of Promise!*
> *It is the Great Mother who giveth birth to Him;*
> *It is the Lord of Life who is born again;*
> *Darkness and tears are set aside when the Sun shall come up early!"*

The Maiden pauses in her declamation, and the High Priestess rises to her feet, drawing the High Priest to his feet. If she is veiled, she throws the veil back from her face. High Priestess and High Priest face each other, clasping each other's crossed-over hands, and start to spin deosil inside the coven. The coven's circling becomes joyous and faster.

The Maiden continues:

> *"Golden Sun of hill and mountain,*
> *Illumine the land, illumine the world,*
> *Illumine the seas, illumine the rivers,*
> *Sorrows be laid, joy to the world!*
> *Blessed be the Great Goddess,*
> *Without beginning, without ending,*

---

3. Written by Doreen Valiente, with words suggested by a Christmas carol in *Carmina Gadelica*, collected by Alexander Carmichael from Angus Gunn, a cottar of Lewis. (See *Carmina Gadelica*, volume I, page 133, or *The Sun Dances*, page 91.) "It was the first chant or invocation I ever wrote for Gerald," Doreen tells us—at Yule 1953, she thinks. He gave her the task of writing words for the evening ritual without warning, after lunch, "deliberately throwing me in at the deep end to see what I could do".

Everlasting to eternity, Io Evo! He![4] *Blessed be!*
Io Evo! He! Blessed be!
Io Evo! He! Blessed be! . . ."

The coven joins in the chant "*Ivo Evo! He! Blessed be!*", and the Maiden puts down her script and candle and joins the circling ring. The chanting and circling continues until the High Priestess cries "*Down!*"

When all are seated, the High Priest stands up again and goes to the altar to fetch a candle or taper. He carries it to the cauldron and with it lights the candle in the cauldron. He then returns the first candle or taper to the altar. If there is a Christmas tree with lights, he now switches on the lights.

He then takes his place in front of the altar, where the High Priestess joins him, and they stand facing the seated coven.

The High Priestess says:

"*Now, at the depth of winter, is the waning of the year accomplished, and the reign of the Holly King is ended. The Sun is reborn, and the waxing of the year begins. The Oak King must slay his brother the Holly King and rule over my land until the height of summer, when his brother shall rise again.*"

The coven stand and, except for the two Kings, withdraw to the perimeter. In the centre of the Circle, the two Kings stand facing each other, the Oak King with his back to the West and the Holly King with his back to the East.

The Oak King places his hands on the Holly King's shoulders, pressing downwards. The Holly King falls to his knees. Meanwhile the Maiden fetches the scarf, and she and the Oak King blindfold the Holly King. They both now move away from the kneeling Holly King; the High Priestess walks slowly round him deosil, three times. She then rejoins the High Priest in front of the altar.

The High Priest says:

"*The spirit of the Holly King is gone from us, to rest in Caer Arianrhod, the Castle of the Silver Wheel; until, with the turning of the year, the season shall come when he shall return to rule again. The*

---

4. Pronounced 'Yo ayvo, hay' (the 'ay' as in 'day'). A Greek Bacchanalian cry. For some thoughts on its possible sexual significance, see Doreen Valiente's *Natural Magic*, p. 92.

spirit is gone; therefore let the man among us who has stood for that spirit be freed from his task."

The High Priestess and Maiden step forward again and help the Holly King to rise. They lead him to the West candle, where the Maiden removes his blindfold and the High Priestess his crown, laying them beside the candle. The man turns and again becomes an ordinary member of the coven.

The Great Rite is now enacted, the Maiden standing by with the athame and the Oak King with the chalice. (If the Sabbat is skyclad, the Maiden will first help the High Priestess to take off her tabard—which, being white, may then suitably be used as the veil laid over her body for the first part of the Great Rite.)

After the wine and cakes, the cauldron is moved to the centre of the Circle, and everybody jumps over it in the usual manner before the party-stage begins.

Next day, when the fire (if any) is cold, the ashes of the Yule Log should be gathered up and scattered on the fields or garden—or, if you live in town and have not even a window-box, on the nearest park or cultivated ground.

Birth, Marriage & Death

XII   Wiccaning

This is a book of suggested rituals for those who need to use them and who find them suitable. It is therefore not the place to debate the difficult question of the religious upbringing of children. But we think one point should be made.

Christians, when they have their children christened, do so on the whole with the intention of *committing* them to Christianity, preferably for life—and to the parents' own particular brand of Christianity, at that. The usual hope is that the children will endorse that commitment at confirmation, when they are old enough to acquiesce consciously (though without mature judgement). To be fair, such parents—when they are not merely following social convention—often act in this way because they sincerely believe it is essential for the safety of their children's souls. They have been taught to believe it and often frightened into believing it. (A young Christian friend of ours, heavily pregnant, was warned by the doctor that the child might be born dead; she sobbed in our arms, terrified that her baby would go to Hell if it did not live long enough to be baptized. She was theologically mistaken even in terms of her own creed; but her terror was all too typical. We are glad to say that her baby son, though late, was born fine and healthy.)

This belief, that there is only one kind of ticket to Heaven and that a baby must be given it with all speed for its own safety, is of course alien to Wicca. Witches' belief in reincarnation denies it in any case. But quite apart from that, witches hold the view which was virtually universal before the era of patriarchal monotheism—namely, that all religions are different ways of expressing the same truths and that their validity for any particular individual depends on his nature and needs.

A wiccaning ceremony for the child of a witch family does not, therefore, commit the child to any one path, even a Wiccan one. It is similar to a christening in that it invokes Divine protection for the child and ritually affirms the love and care with which the family and friends wish to surround the newcomer. It differs from a christening in that it specifically acknowledges that, as the child matures into an adult, it will, and indeed must, decide on its own path.

Wicca is above all a natural religion—so witch parents will naturally try to communicate to their children the joy and fulfilment their religion gives them, and the whole family will inevitably share in its way of life. Sharing is one thing; imposing or dictating is another, and, far from ensuring a child's 'salvation', may well retard it—if, as witches do, you regard salvation not as a kind of instant transaction but as a development over many lifetimes.

We have composed our wiccaning ritual in this spirit, and we think that most witches will agree with the attitude.

We knew that the idea of having godparents—adult friends who will take a continuing personal interest in the child's development—was a justifiably popular one; and we felt that a wiccaning ceremony should allow for it too. At first we called these adult friends 'sponsors', to avoid confusion with Christian practice. But on further consideration we saw that 'sponsor' was a cold word and that there was no reason at all why 'godfather' and 'godmother' (if 'god' be taken to include 'goddess') should not serve for witches as well as Christians. After all, given the differences of belief (and Christians differ among themselves, God knows), including the difference of attitude we have already mentioned, the function is the same.

Godparents do not necessarily have to be witches themselves; that is up to the parents. But they must at least be in sympathy with the intent of the rite and have read it through beforehand, to make sure they can make the necessary promises in all sincerity. (The same would apply, after all, to witches who were asked by Christian friends to be godparents at a church baptism.)

If the High Priestess and/or High Priest are themselves standing as godparents, they will make the promises to each other at the appropriate moments in the ritual.

There is a story attached to this ritual of ours which is both funny and sad. We wrote it originally in 1971, and we gave a copy to a High Priest friend who we thought might like to have it. A couple of years later, an American witch friend was visiting us, and we happened to describe our wiccaning to him in conversation. He laughed and said: "But I've read that ritual. Last time I was in London, —— showed it to me. He said he'd got it from a very old traditional source."

By such irresponsibility are apocryphal stories launched; and they do no good to Wicca at all. Besides, we have since amended the ritual slightly in the light of experience—so will people who know of the original now accuse us of 'tampering with tradition'? It could happen!

Following Wiccan patterns, we have suggested that the High Priest should preside at the wiccaning of a girl child, and the High Priestess at that of a boy. To avoid lengthy repetition, we give the ritual for a girl child in full, and then indicate the differences for a boy child.

The Preparation

If the coven normally works skyclad, the decision whether the ritual shall be skyclad or robed shall on this occasion rest with the parents. In either case, the High Priestess shall wear symbols of the Moon, and the High Priest symbols of the Sun.

The Circle is marked with flowers and greenery, and the cauldron placed in the centre, filled with the same, and perhaps with fruit as well.

Consecrating oil is placed ready on the altar.

Only very light incense should be used—preferably joss-sticks.

Gifts for the child are placed beside the altar, and food and drink for a little party in the Circle after the ritual.

The parents should choose beforehand a 'hidden name' for the child. (This is largely for the child's own benefit; growing up in a witch family, he or she will almost certainly like having a private 'witch name' just as Mummy and Daddy do—and if not, it can be quietly forgotten until and unless its owner wants to use it again.)

The Ritual for a Girl Child

The Opening Ritual proceeds as usual up to the end of the "Great God Cernunnos" invocation, except that everyone, including the parents and child, is in the Circle before the casting, seated in a semicircle close to the cauldron and facing towards the altar—leaving room for the High Priestess to cast the Circle around them. Only the High Priestess and High Priest are standing, to conduct the Opening Ritual. To cut down excessive movement which might frighten the child, the High Priestess casts the Circle with her athame, not the sword; and nobody moves with her, or copies her gestures, when she invokes the Lords of the Watchtowers. She and the High Priest carry round the elements.

After the *"Great God Cernunnos"* invocation, the High Priestess and High Priest consecrate the wine. They do not taste it but place the chalice on the altar.

The High Priest then stands before the altar, facing the cauldron. The High Priestess stands ready to hand him the oil, wine and water.

The High Priest says:

"We are met in this Circle to ask the blessing of the mighty God and the gentle Goddess on ——, the daughter of —— and ——, so that she may grow in beauty and strength, in joy and wisdom. There are many paths, and each must find his own; therefore we do not seek to bind —— to any one path while she is still too young to choose.

Rather do we ask the God and the Goddess, who know all paths, and to whom all paths lead, to bless, protect and prepare her through the years of her childhood; so that when at last she is truly grown, she shall know without doubt or fear which path is hers and shall tread it gladly.

"——, mother of ——, bring her forward that she may be blessed."

The father helps the mother to rise, and both of them bring the child to the High Priest, who takes her in his arms (firmly, or she will feel insecure—too many clergymen make that mistake!). He asks:

"——, mother of ——, has this your child also a hidden name?"

The mother replies:

"Her hidden name is——."

The High Priest then anoints the child on the forehead with oil, marking a pentagram and saying:

"I anoint thee, —— (ordinary name), *with oil, and give thee the hidden name of——."*

He repeats the action with wine, saying:

"I anoint thee, —— (hidden name), *with wine, in the name of the mighty God Cernunnos."*

He repeats the action with water, saying:

"I anoint thee, —— (hidden-name), *with water, in the name of the gentle Goddess Aradia."*

The High Priest gives the child back to the mother and then leads the parents and child to each of the Watchtowers in turn, saying:

"Ye Lords of the Watchtowers of the East (South, West, North), we do bring before you ——, whose hidden name is ——, and who has been duly anointed within the Wiccan Circle. Hear ye, therefore, that she is under the protection of Cernunnos and Aradia."

The High Priest and High Priestess take their places facing the altar, with the parents and child between them. They raise their arms and call in turn:

High Priest: *"Mighty Cernunnos, bestow upon this child the gift of strength."*

High Priestess: *"Gentle Aradia, bestow upon this child the gift of beauty."*

High Priest: *"Mighty Cernunnos, bestow upon this child the gift of wisdom."*

High Priestess: "*Gentle Aradia, bestow upon this child the gift of love.*"

The High Priest, High Priestess and parents turn to face into the Circle, and the High Priest then asks:

"*Are there two in the Circle who would stand as godparents to* ——?"

(If he and the High Priestess are standing as godparents, he will ask instead: "*Is there one in the Circle who will stand with me, as godparents to* ——?" and the High Priestess answers: "*I will join with you.*" They then face each other and speak the questions and the promises to each other.)

The godparents come forward and stand, the godmother facing the High Priest, and the godfather facing the High Priestess.

The High Priest asks the godmother:

"*Do you,* ——, *promise to be a friend to* —— *throughout her childhood, to aid and guide her as she shall need; and in concord with her parents, to watch over her and love her as if she were of your own blood, till by the grace of Cernunnos and Aradia she shall be ready to choose her own path?*"

The godmother replies:

"*I,* ——, *do so promise.*"

The High Priestess asks the godfather:

"*Do you,* ——, *promise . . .*" etc., as above.

The godfather replies:

"*I,* ——, *do so promise.*"

The High Priest says:

> "*The God and the Goddess have blessed her;*
> *The Lords of the Watchtowers have acknowledged her;*
> *We her friends have welcomed her;*
> *Therefore, O Circle of Stars,*
> *Shine in peace on*——,
> *Whose hidden name is*——.
> *So mote it be.*"

All say:

"*So mote it be.*"

The High Priest says:

"*Let all be seated within the Circle.*"

All sit down, except the High Priest and High Priestess, who taste and pass round the already-consecrated wine in the usual way and then consecrate and pass round the cakes in the usual way.

They then fetch the gifts and the party food and drink and sit down with the others, and the proceedings become informal.

The Ritual for a Boy Child

The basic difference if the child is a boy is that the High Priest and High Priestess exchange duties. She makes the opening statement and performs the anointing, the High Priest handing her the oil, wine and water. She presents the child to the Watchtowers.

The call to the God and Goddess for their gifts of strength, beauty, wisdom and love, however, is made exactly as for a girl child, and in the same order.

The High Priestess calls forward the godparents and takes the godfather's promise; the High Priest then takes the god-mother's promise.

The High Priestess pronounces the final blessing.

XIII   Handfasting

A handfasting is a witch wedding. Stewart has explained handfasting at some length in Chapter 15 of *What Witches do*, so we will not repeat that explanation here. All the widely differing versions of handfasting ritual which we have come across (including the one outlined in *What Witches Do*) have been devised in recent years and are a mixture of bits of tradition (such as jumping the broomstick) with the devisers' own ideas. So far as we know, no detailed and provably ancient handfasting ritual exists on paper.

So when we were asked to conduct a handfasting for two of our members a few days after their legal marriage, we decided that we too would write our own, since none of the ones we knew of quite satisfied us.

Like many other witches and occultists, we have found Dion

Fortune's unforgettable novel *The Sea Priestess* (Aquarian Press, London, 1957) a goldmine of material for devised rituals and have benefited from the results. So, for our friends' hand-fasting, we incorporated some of the Priest of the Moon's words to Molly in Chapter XXX of *The Sea Priestess*;[1] we felt they might almost have been written for the purpose. They are the four quotations below from "*Golden Aphrodite cometh not as the virgin . . .*" down to "*they become the substance of the sacrament*". Our only alteration of the original has been to substitute "*bride*" for "*priestess*" at one point; this seemed a legitimate amendment for a handfasting ritual.

These passages are included here by kind permission of the Society of the Inner Light, who hold the copyright of Dion Fortune's works. Responsibility for the context in which they have been used is, of course, entirely ours and not the Society's; but we like to think that, if the late Miss Fortune had been able to be present, we would have had her blessing.

One other point: in the presentation of the symbols of the elements, we attribute the Wand to Air, and the Sword to Fire. (See Plate 18.) This is the tradition which we follow—but others attribute the Wand to Fire and the Sword to Air. The Wand/Fire, Sword/Air attribution was a deliberate 'blind' perpetrated by the early Golden Dawn, which has unfortunately not yet died a natural death; it seems to us contrary to the obvious nature of the tools concerned. However, many people have been brought up to believe that the 'blind' was the genuine tradition, so that by now, for them, it feels right. They should of course amend the wording of the presentation accordingly.

The Preparation

The Circle is outlined, and the altar decorated, with flowers; but a gateway is left in the North-East of the Circle, with flowers to hand for closing it.

The broomstick is kept ready beside the altar.

The cauldron, filled with flowers, is placed by the West candle—West representing Water, the element of love.

---

1. Chapter 14 of the paperback edition (Star, London, 1976).

The Ritual

The Opening Ritual is conducted normally, except that (a) the bride and groom remain outside the gateway, which is not closed yet, and (b) the Charge is not given yet.

After the "*Great God Cernunnos*" invocation, the High Priestess brings in the groom, and the High Priest the bride, each with a kiss. The High Priest then closes the gateway with flowers, and the High Priestess closes it ritually with the sword or athame.

The High Priestess and High Priest stand with their backs to the altar. The groom faces the High Priestess, and the bride the High Priest, in the centre of the Circle.

The High Priestess asks:

"*Who comes to be joined together in the presence of the Goddess? What is thy name, O Man?*"

The groom answers:

"*My name is ——.*"

The High Priest asks:

"*Who comes to be joined together in the presence of the God? What is thy name, O Woman?*"

The bride answers:

"*My name is ——.*"

The High Priestess says:

"*—— and ——, we greet you with joy.*"

The coven circle round the bride and groom to the Witches' Rune; then all return to their places.

The High Priestess says:

"*Unity is balance, and balance is unity. Hear then, and understand.*"

She picks up the wand and continues:

"*The wand that I hold is the symbol of Air. Know and remember that this is the element of Life, of intelligence, of the inspiration which moves us onwards. By this wand of Air, we bring to your handfasting the power of Mind.*"

She lays down the wand. The High Priest picks up the sword and says:

"*The sword that I hold is the symbol of Fire. Know and remember that this is the element of Light, of energy, of the vigour which runs through our veins. By this sword of Fire, we bring to your handfasting the power of Will.*"

He lays down the sword. The High Priestess picks up the chalice and says:

"The chalice that I hold is the symbol of Water. Know and remember, that this is the element of Love, of growth, of the fruitfulness of the Great Mother. By this chalice of Water, we bring to your handfasting the power of Desire."

She lays down the chalice. The High Priest picks up the pentacle and says:

"The pentacle that I hold is the symbol of Earth. Know and remember, that this is the element of Law, of endurance, of the understanding which cannot be shaken. By this pentacle of Earth, we bring to your handfasting the power of the Steadfast."

He lays down the pentacle, and continues;

"Listen to the words of the Great Mother . . ." etc., to introduce the Charge.

The High Priestess and the High Priest deliver the Charge, in the usual way. When it is finished, the High Priest says:

"Golden Aphrodite cometh not as the virgin, the victim, but as the Awakener, the Desirous One. As outer space she calls, and the All-Father commences the courtship. She awakeneth Him to desire, and the worlds are created. How powerful is she, golden Aphrodite, the awakener of manhood!"

The High Priestess says:

"But all these things are one thing. All the goddesses are one goddess, and we call her Isis, the All-woman, in whose nature all natural things are found; virgin and desirous by turn; giver of life and bringer-in of death. She is the cause of all creation, for she awakeneth the desire of the All-Father, and for her sake He createth. Likewise, the wise call all women Isis."

The High Priest says:

"In the face of every woman, let man look for the features of the Great Goddess, watching her phases through the flow and return of the tides to which his soul answereth; listening for her call."

The High Priestess says:

"O daughter of Isis, adore the Goddess, and in her name give the call that awakens and rejoices. So shalt thou be blessed of the Goddess, and live with the fulness of life. Let the Bride show forth the Goddess to him who loves her. Let her assume the crown of the underworld. Let her arise all glorious and golden from the sea of the primordial and call unto him to come forth, to come to her. Let her do ·

*these things in the name of the Goddess, and she shall be even as the
Goddess unto him; for the Goddess will speak through her. All-
powerful shall she be on the Inner, as crowned Persephone; and
all-powerful on the Outer, as golden Aphrodite.[2] So shall she be a
priestess in the eyes of the worshipper of the Goddess, who by his faith
and dedication shall find the Goddess in her. For the rite of Isis is life,
and that which is done as a rite shall show forth in life. By the rite is
the Goddess drawn down to her worshippers; her power enters into
them, and they become the substance of the sacrament."*

The High Priest says to the bride:

*"Say after me: 'By seed and root, by bud and stem, by leaf and
flower and fruit, by life and love, in the name of the Goddess, I,
——, take thee, ——, to my hand, my heart and my spirit, at the
setting of the sun and the rising of the stars.[3] Nor shall death part us;
for in the fulness of time we shall be born again at the same time and
in the same place as each other; and we shall meet, and know, and
remember, and love again.'"*

The bride repeats each phrase after the High Priest, taking
the groom's right hand in her own right hand as she speaks.

The High Priestess says to the groom:

"Say after me: 'By seed and root, by bud and stem . . .'" etc., as
above.

The groom repeats each phrase after the High Priestess,
retaining the bride's right hand in his own.

If the couple wish to exchange rings, this is now done.

The High Priest says:

*"Let the sun and the moon and the stars, and these our brothers
and sisters, bear witness; that —— and —— have been joined*

---

2. We cannot resist noting here a belief that still lingers in the gale-prone West
of Ireland—that a newly-wed bride has the power to calm a storm at sea. As a
neighbour (living, like ourselves, a mile from the Atlantic) said to us: "I
believe there may be some truth in it. A bride has a certain blessing about
her."

3. At their own discretion, the couple may end their pledge here, omitting the
last sentence from *"Nor shall death part us . . ."* if they do not yet see their way
to a soul-mate commitment, which should never be undertaken without
careful thought. (See *What Witches Do*, Chapter 15.) The Mormon Church,
incidentally, has the same provision; Mormons have two forms of marriage—
one for life, and the other (called "Going to the Temple") for eternity. About
fifty per cent choose the latter form.

*together in the sight of the God and the Goddess. And may the God
and the Goddess bless them, as we do ourselves.''*

All say:

"So mote it be!''

The High Priestess takes the broomstick and lays it down on
the ground before the couple, who jump over it hand in hand.
The High Priestess then picks up the broomstick and ritually
sweeps the Circle clear of all evil influences.

The couple now enact the Great Rite, and it is entirely their
choice whether it should be symbolic or actual. If it is actual, the
High Priestess leads the coven out of the room, instead of the
Maiden as is usual.

After the Great Rite, the couple consecrate the wine and
cakes (or the cakes only if the Great Rite has been symbolic, in
which case the wine will already have been consecrated). The
proceedings then become informal.

If the feast includes a handfasting cake, tradition says that
this is the one occasion when the coven's ritual sword may be
used for actual cutting.

XIV Requiem

The first time we lost a coven-member by death, this is the Requiem we held for her. 'Lost' is an inappropriate word, of course; her contribution to the building of our group mind remained, and in our incarnations to come we may well be drawn together again. But the ending of a chapter needs to be acknowledged and absorbed, and the urge to say *au revoir* with love and dignity has been universal since Neanderthal man laid his dead to rest on a couch of blossom.

Two symbolic themes seemed to us to express what we wanted to say. The first was the spiral, which since the very dawn of ritual has stood for the parallel processes of death-rebirth and initiation-rebirth; winding our way back to the source, the universal womb, the Great Mother, the depths of the collective unconscious—meeting the Dark Mother face to face and knowing that she is also the Bright Mother—and then winding our way outwards from the encounter rejuvenated and transformed. This inward and outward spiral naturally took the form of a dance; and the inward spiral seemed again to call for that rare use of a widdershins movement, employed in Wiccan ritual only when it has a precise symbolic purpose (as in our Autumn Equinox and Samhain rituals). It would be followed naturally by a deosil movement for the outward spiral.

The other theme was that of the silver cord. Time and again, people who have experienced astral projection have spoken of this silver cord, which they have seen weaving, and infinitely extendable, between the astral and the physical bodies. On physical death, all traditions maintain, the cord is severed. This is a natural process, the first stage in the withdrawal of the immortal Individuality from the physical, lower and upper astral, and lower mental bodies of the Personality which has housed it during one incarnation. Any blocking or interruption of this withdrawal is a malfunction, as abnormality; it may be caused by some obsession, and this explains many 'hauntings'. In most cases (certainly, we think, in that of our friend) there is no such undue retardation. But even if no help is needed to smooth the withdrawal, it is fitting that it should be symbolized in the rite.

Tradition also maintains that the beautiful words of Ecclesiastes xii, 6–7, refer to this process; so we used them in our Requiem, substituting 'Goddess' for 'God'—which, in view of our declared philosophy, we hope will offend no one.

The second part of the ritual is the enacting of the Legend of the Descent of the Goddess into the Underworld, which appears in the Book of Shadows as a kind of epilogue to the second-degree initiation ritual. Where Gardner obtained it, not even Doreen Valiente knows. "I had nothing whatever to do with writing this," she tells us. "Whether old Gerald wrote it himself or whether he inherited it, I do not know. I suspect a bit of both, namely that he inherited the rough outlines of it and wrote it down in his own words. It is, as you say, a version of the Ishtar story and similar legends; and it relates to the initiation ritual in obvious ways."

Initiation and rebirth are closely parallel processes, so we found that the Legend enriched our Requiem as it does the second-degree rite. The spoken words of the Legend are given in *What Witches Do* and (in slightly shorter form) in Gardner's *Witchcraft Today*, but we repeat them for completeness, interspersed with the appropriate movements, which the Book of Shadows leaves to the imagination. If the Legend is enacted at all frequently—and there is no need to confine it to the second-degree initiation, we have found that it is easy, and worth while, to learn them. To get the most out of the Legend, it is even better if the three actors learn the dialogue parts of it by heart and speak them themselves, instead of leaving all the speaking to the Narrator as we have done below. But unless they know them by heart, it is better to leave them to the Narrator, because for the three actors to carry books in their hands spoils the whole effect.

Finally, the High Priestess announces the love-feast, with a closing valediction to the dead friend.

We would like to make one comment on the rite as we first experienced it. The moment of the breaking of the bowl had an unexpected impact on all of us; it was as though it echoed on all the planes at once. Our youngest member gasped out loud, and we all felt like it. A sceptic might say that the sharp sound of the breaking, charged with symbolism as it was, provided a psychological shock; but even if this were all, it would still be valid—concentrating our group awareness of the meaning of what we were doing into one intense and simultaneous instant.

When the ritual was over, we felt a calm happiness none of us had known since our friend became ill. Seldom have we been so aware of a ritual's being successful and reverberating majestically far beyond the limits of our Circle.

In the text below, we have used 'she' throughout, for simplicity. If the Requiem is used for a man, it may be felt appropriate to exchange the roles of High Priest and High Priestess for the first part of the ritual, up to the Legend; as always, it is a matter of what feels right to the coven concerned.

The Preparation

The decoration of the Circle and the altar for a Requiem will be a matter of individual taste, depending upon the circumstances, the time of year and the character and associations of the friend being remembered.

A small earthenware bowl (a mug or cup with a handle is suitable) is laid beside the altar, with a silver cord tied to it; also a hammer for breaking the bowl, and a cloth to break it in.

For the Legend of the Descent of the Goddess, jewels and a veil are laid ready by the altar for the Goddess, and a crown for the Lord of the Underworld. A necklace is laid ready on the altar.

The Ritual

The opening ritual proceeds as usual, up to the end of the *"Great God Cernunnos"* invocation. The High Priestess and High Priest then face the coven from in front of the altar.

The High Priestess says:

"We meet today in both sadness and joy. We are sad because a chapter has closed; yet are we joyful, because, by the closing, a new chapter may begin.

"We meet to mark the passing of our beloved sister, ——, for whom this incarnation is ended. We meet to commend her to the care of blessing of the God and the Goddess, that she may rest, free from illusion or regret, until the time shall come for her rebirth to this world. And knowing that this shall be so, we know, too, that the sadness is nothing and that the joy is all."

The High Priest stays in his place, and the High Priestess leads the coven in a spiral dance, slowly inwards in a widdershins direction, but not closing in too tightly.

The High Priest says:

"We call to thee, Ama, dark sterile Mother; thou to whom all manifested life must return, when its time has come; dark Mother of stillness and rest, before whom men tremble because they understand thee not. We call to thee, who art also Hecate of the waning Moon, dark Lady of wisdom, whom men fear because thy wisdom towers above their own. We, the hidden children of the Goddess, know that there is naught to fear in thine embrace, which none escape; that when we step into thy darkness, as all must, it is but to step again into the light. Therefore, in love and without fear, we commend to thee ——, our sister. Take her, guard her, guide her; admit her to the peace of the Summerlands, which stand between life and life. And know, as thou knowest all things, that our love goes with her."

The High Priest fetches the bowl, cord, hammer and cloth. The dance stops, and the coven part to admit the High Priest to the centre of the spiral, where he lays the cloth on the floor and the bowl upon it. He hands the free end of the cord to the Maiden.

The High Priestess says:

"Or ever the silver cord be loosed, or the golden bowl be broken, or the pitcher be broken at the fountain, or the wheel be broken at the cistern; then shall the dust return to the earth as it was; and the spirit shall return to the Goddess who gave it."

The High Priest unties the silver cord, and the Maiden gathers it up. The High Priest then wraps the cloth around the bowl and breaks it with the hammer. He replaces the folded cloth with the pieces of the bowl in it, and the hammer, beside the altar. The coven re-closes.

The Maiden carries the silver cord and, during the following invocation, proceeding deosil round the Circle, offers it first to the Lords of the Watchtowers of the West (the Lords of Death and of Initiation) and then to the Lords of the Watchtowers of the East (the Lords of Rebirth). She then lays the cord on the floor in front of the East candle and joins the High Priest at the altar (proceeding always deosil).

Meanwhile the High Priestess leads the dance again, doubling back deosil to unwind the spiral, until it is once again a full circle, which continues to move deosil.

As soon as he has replaced the cloth and hammer beside the altar, the High Priest faces the coven and says:

"We call to thee, Aima, bright fertile Mother; thou who art the womb of rebirth, from whom all manifested life proceeds, and at whose flowing breast all are nourished. We call to thee, who art also Persephone of the waxing Moon, Lady of Springtime and of all things new. We commend to thee ——, our sister. Take her, guard her, guide her; bring her in the fulness of time to a new birth and a new life. And grant that in that new life she may be loved again, as we her brothers and sisters have loved her."

The High Priest and the Maiden rejoin the circling coven, and the High Priestess starts the Witches' Rune, which the rest join in. When it is over, the High Priestess orders *"Down"*, and the coven sit in a ring facing inwards.

The High Priestess then allots roles for the Legend of the Descent of the Goddess into the Underworld: the Narrator, the Goddess, the Lord of the Underworld and the Guardian of the Portals. The Goddess is adorned with jewellery and veiled and stands at the edge of the Circle in the South-East. The Lord of the Underworld puts on his crown, takes up the sword and stands with his back to the altar. The Guardian of the Portals takes up his athame and the red cord and stands facing the Goddess.

The Narrator says:

"In ancient times, our Lord, the Hornéd One, was (as he still is) the Consoler, the Comforter. But men knew him as the dread Lord of Shadows, lonely, stern and just. But our Lady the Goddess would solve all mysteries, even the mystery of death; and so she journeyed to the Underworld. The Guardian of the Portals challenged her. . . ."

The Guardian of the Portals challenges the Goddess with his athame.

". . . 'Strip off thy garments, lay aside thy jewels; for naught mayest thou bring with thee into this our land.'"[1]

The Goddess takes off her veil and jewellery; nothing must be left on her. (If the Requiem is robed, only her plain robe must be left on her.) He then binds her with the red cord in the manner of the first-degree initiation, with the centre of the cord round the front of her neck, and the ends passed over her shoulders to tie her wrists together behind her waist.

"So she laid down her garments and her jewels and was bound, as all living must be who seek to enter the realms of Death, the Mighty One."

The Guardian of the Portals leads the Goddess to stand facing the Lord of the Underworld. The Guardian then steps aside.

"Such was her beauty that Death himself knelt, and laid his sword and crown at her feet. . . ."

The Lord of the Underworld kneels before the Goddess (see Plate 20), lays his sword and his crown on the ground on each side of her, then kisses her right foot and her left foot.

". . . and kissed her feet, saying: 'Blessed be thy feet, that have brought thee in these ways. Abide with me; but let me place my cold hands on thy heart.'"

The Lord of the Underworld raises his hands, palms forward, and holds them a few inches from the Goddess's heart.

---

1. Since all the words of the Legend are spoken by the Narrator, we have not repeated "The Narrator says" each time. If the three actors can speak their own lines from memory, so much the better.

"And she replied: 'I love thee not. Why dost thou cause all things that I love, and take delight in, to fade and die?'"

The Lord of the Underworld spreads his arms outwards and downwards, with the palms of his hands forward.

"'Lady,' replied Death, 'it is age and fate, against which I am helpless. Age causes all things to wither; but when men die at the end of time, I give them rest and peace and strength, so that they may return. But thou, thou art lovely; return not, abide with me.' But she answered: 'I love thee not.'"

The Lord of the Underworld rises, goes to the altar and picks up the scourge. He turns to face the Goddess.

"Then said Death: 'An thou receivest not my hands on thy heart, thou must kneel to Death's scourge.' 'It is fate—better so,' she said, and she knelt. And Death scourged her tenderly."

The Goddess kneels, facing the altar. The Lord of the Underworld gives her three, seven, nine and twenty-one very gentle strokes of the scourge.

"And she cried: 'I know the pangs of love.'"

The Lord of the Underworld replaces the scourge on the altar, helps the Goddess to rise and kneels facing her.

"And Death raised her, and said: 'Blessed be.' And he gave her the Fivefold Kiss, saying: 'Thus only mayest thou attain to joy and knowledge.'"

The Lord of the Underworld gives the Goddess the Fivefold Kiss (but without the usual spoken words). He then unties her wrists, laying the cord on the ground.

"And he taught her all his mysteries and gave her the necklace which is the circle of rebirth."

The Lord of the Underworld fetches the necklace from the altar and places it round the Goddess's neck. The Goddess then takes up the crown and replaces it on the Lord of the Underworld's head.

"And she taught him the mystery of the sacred cup, which is the cauldron of rebirth."

The Lord of the Underworld moves in front of the altar at its East end, and the Goddess moves in front of the altar at its West end. The Goddess picks up the chalice in both her hands, they face each other, and he places both his hands round hers.

"They loved, and were one; for there be three great mysteries in the life of man, and magic controls them all. To fulfil love, you must

return again at the same time and at the same place as the loved ones; and you must meet, and know, and remember, and love them again."

The Lord of the Underworld releases the Goddess's hands, and she replaces the chalice on the altar. He picks up the scourge in his left hand and the sword in his right and stands in the God Position, forearms crossed on his breast and sword and scourge pointing upwards, with his back to the altar. She stands beside him in the Goddess Position, feet astride and arms outstretched to form the Pentagram.

"*But to be reborn, you must die, and be made ready for a new body. And to die, you must be born; and without love, you may not be born. And our Goddess ever inclineth to love, and mirth, and happiness; and she guardeth and cherisheth her hidden children in life, and in death she teacheth the way to her communion; and even in this world she teacheth them the mystery of the Magic Circle, which is placed between the worlds of men and of the Gods.*"

The Lord of the Underworld replaces the scourge, sword and crown on or by the altar. This completes the Legend, and the actors rejoin the rest of the coven.

The High Priestess says:

"*Let us now, as the Goddess hath taught us, share the love-feast of the wine and the cakes; and as we do so, let us remember our sister ———, with whom we have so often shared it.*[2] *And with this communion, we lovingly place our sister in the hands of the Goddess.*"

All say:

"*So mote it be.*"

The wine and cakes are consecrated and passed round.

As soon as practicable after the Requiem, the pieces of the bowl are ritually thrown into a running stream or river, with the traditional command: "Return to the elements from which thou camest."[3]

---

2. If the Requiem is for a non-witch friend, or for a witch who was not a member of the coven, the phrase "with whom we have so often shared it" is of course omitted.

3. Any ritually-used object which has served its purpose and will not be needed for further working—especially if, like the Requiem bowl, it has been linked with an individual—must be ritually neutralized and disposed of; it is irresponsible, and may be dangerous, to allow it to linger. The running-water method is a time-honoured and satisfactory ritual of disposal.

Bibliography

It would be impossible to name all the books that have helped us in our study of the Eight Festivals and the concepts that lie behind them; but the following is a list of those we have found particularly informative, illuminating or even provocative. It also includes all books mentioned in the text. The editions named are not always the first ones, but are those we have used or have found to be currently available.

ASHE, GEOFFREY—*The Virgin* (Routledge & Kegan Paul, London, 1976)

BUCKLAND, RAYMOND—*The Tree, the Complete Book of Saxon Witchcraft* (Samuel Weiser, New York, 1974)

BURLAND, C. A.—*The Magical Arts, a Short History* (Arthur Barker, London, 1966)

CARMICHAEL, ALEXANDER—*Carmina Gadelica, Hymns and Incantations, with Illustrative Notes of Words, Rites and Customs Dying and Obsolete* (Oliver & Boyd, Edinburgh); volumes I and II, 1900; 2nd edition, volumes I–VI, 1928 onwards.

CARMICHAEL, ALEXANDER—*The Sun Dances* (Floris Books, Edinburgh, 1977). A paperback selection from the English translations contained in *Carmina Gadelica*.

CLÉBERT, JEAN-PAUL—*The Gypsies* (English translation by Charles Duff, Vista Books, London, 1963)

CROWLEY, ALEISTER—*777 Revised* (Neptune Press, London, 1952)

CROWLEY, ALEISTER—*Magick* (Routledge & Kegan Paul, London, 1973)

CULPEPER, NICHOLAS—*Culpeper's Complete Herbal* (mid-seventeenth century; current edition W. Foulsham & Co., London & New York, undated)

DILLON, MYLES & CHADWICK, NORA—*The Celtic Realms* (Weidenfeld & Nicolson, London, 1967)

DINNEEN, REV. PATRICK S.—*Foclóir Gaedhilge agus Béarla—An Irish-English Dictionary* (Irish Texts Society, Dublin, 1927). Note for Irish scholars: the new Niall O Dónaill *Foclóir Gaeilge-Béarla* (Oifig an tSoláthair, Dublin, 1977) is admirable for modern Irish usage but less informative than Dinneen on mythological and folk-lore references. (See "MacALPINE, NEIL" for Scottish Gaelic.)

DONOVAN, FRANK—*Never on a Broomstick* (Stackpole Books, Harrisburg, Pa., 1971)

DUFFY, MAUREEN—*The Erotic World of Faery* (Hodder & Stoughton, London, 1972)

DURDIN-ROBERTSON, LAWRENCE—*The Cult of the Goddess* (Cesara Publications, Clonegal, Ireland, 1974)

DURDIN-ROBERTSON, LAWRENCE—*The Goddesses of Chaldaea, Syria and Egypt* (Cesara Publications, 1976)

DURDIN-ROBERTSON, LAWRENCE—*The Symbolism of Temple Architecture* (Cesara Publications, 1978)

Encyclopaedia Britannica, 1957 edition.

FARRAR, STEWART—*What Witches Do* (2nd edition, Capel Books, Dublin, 1983, and Phoenix Publications, Custer, WA., 1983). (Spanish translation *Lo que Hacen las Brujas*, Ediciones Martinez Roca, Barcelona, 1977.)

FORTUNE, DION—*The Mystical Qabala* (Rider, London, 1954)

FORTUNE, DION—*The Sea Priestess* (Aquarian Press, London, 1957)

FORTUNE, DION—*Moon Magic* (Aquarian Press, 1956)

FRAZER, SIR J. G.—*The Golden Bough* (*Abridged Edition*) (Macmillan, London, paperback 1974). Our page references are to this reprint, which differs from the 1922 original and is more easily obtained.

GANTZ, JEFFREY (translator)—*The Mabinogion* (Penguin, London, 1976). This paperback is now more easily obtained than the well-known Everyman translation by Gwyn and Thomas Jones (J. M. Dent & Sons, London, 1949)

GARDNER, GERALD B.—*Witchcraft Today* (Rider, London 1954)

GARDNER, GERALD B.—*The Meaning of Witchcraft* (Aquarian Press, London, 1959)

GLASS, JUSTINE—*Witchcraft, the Sixth Sense—and Us* (Neville Spearman, London, 1965)

GRAVES, ROBERT—*The White Goddess* (3rd edition, Faber & Faber, London, 1952)

GRAVES, ROBERT—*The Greek Myths*, two volumes, revised edition (Penguin, London, 1960)

GRAVES, TOM—*Needles of Stone* (Turnstone Books, London, 1978)

GRIGSON, GEOFFREY—*The Goddess of Love: The birth, triumph, death and return of Aphrodite* (Constable, London, 1976)

HARDING, M. ESTHER—*Woman's Mysteries* (Rider, London, 1971)

HARRISON, MICHAEL—*The Roots of Witchcraft* (Frederick Muller, London, 1973)

HAWKES, JACQUETTA—*Dawn of the Gods* (Chatto & Windus, London, 1968)

HERM, GERHARD—*The Celts* (Weidenfeld & Nicolson, London, 1976)

HITCHING, FRANCIS—*Earth Magic* (Cassell, London, 1976)

HUSON, PAUL—*Mastering Witchcraft* (Rupert Hart-Davis, London, 1970)

INWARDS, RICHARD—*Weather Lore* (Rider, London, 1950)

JACKSON, KENNETH (translator)—*A Celtic Miscellany* (Penguin, London, 1971)

JUNG, CARL G.—*Collected Works, volume IX; 2nd edition* (Routledge & Kegan Paul, London, 1968)

JUNG, CARL G.—(editor) *Man and His Symbols* (Aldus Books, London, 1964)

KIPLING, RUDYARD—*Puck of Pook's Hill* (Macmillan, London, 1906)

Larousse Encyclopaedia of Mythology (Hatchworth Press, London, 1959)

LELAND, CHARLES G.—*Aradia: the Gospel of the Witches*, introduced by Stewart Farrar (C. W. Daniel Co., London, 1974)

LETHBRIDGE, T. C.—*Witches: Investigating an Ancient Religion* (Routledge & Kegan Paul, London, 1962)

MacALISTER, R. A. STEWART (editor and translator)—*Lebor Gabála Érenn, the Book of the Taking of Ireland*, Parts I–V (Irish

Texts Society, Dublin, 1938–56). Commonly known as *The Book of Invasions*, this is a collection of mediaeval texts in which monks recorded very much older, originally oral, material.

MacALPINE, NEIL—*Pronouncing Gaelic-English Dictionary* (Gairm Publications, Glasgow, 1973). This for Scottish Gaelic; for Irish, see under "DINNEEN, REV. PATRICK S.".

MacCANA, PROINSIAS—*Celtic Mythology* (Hamlyn, London, 1970)

MacNEILL, MÁIRE—*The Festival of Lughnasa* (Oxford University Press, London, 1962)

MacNIOCAILL, GEARÓID—*Ireland Before the Vikings* (Gill & Macmillan, Dublin, 1972)

MARKALE, JEAN—*Women of the Celts* (Gordon Cremonesi, London, 1975)

MARTELLO, Dr LEO LOUIS—*Witchcraft, the Old Religion* (University Press, Secausus N. J., undated)

MATHERS, S. LIDELL MacGREGOR (translator and editor)—*The Key of Solomon the King (Clavicula Salomonis)*, with foreword by Richard Cavendish (Routledge & Kegan Paul, London, 1972). (The original Mathers edition was published by George Redway in 1888.)

MICHELL, JOHN—*The Earth Spirit, its Ways, Shrines, and Mysteries* (Thames & Hudson, London, and Avon Books, New York, 1975)

MURRAY, MARGARET A.—*The Witch-Cult in Western Europe* (Oxford University Press, London, 1921)

MURRAY, MARGARET A.—*The God of the Witches* (Daimon Press, Castle Hedingham, Essex, 1962)

MURRAY, MARGARET A.—*The Splendour that was Egypt* (revised edition, Sidgwick & Jackson, London, 1964)

NEUMANN, ERICH—*The Great Mother* (2nd edition, Routledge & Kegan Paul, London, 1963)

OVID—*Fasti*, Henry T. Riley's translation (Bell & Daldy, London, 1870)

REES, ALWYN & BRINLEY—*Celtic Heritage* (Thames & Hudson, London, 1961)

REGARDIE, ISRAEL—*The Golden Dawn* (four volumes, 3rd edition, Hazel Hills Corpn., River Falls, Wisconsin, 1970)

ROSS, ANNE—*Pagan Celtic Britain* (Routledge & Kegan Paul, London, 1974)

SEYMOUR, St. JOHN D.—*Irish Witchcraft and Demonology* (1913; reprinted by E. P. Publishing Co, East Ardsley, Yorkshire, 1972)

"SHEBA, LADY", who claims to be America's Witch Queen, is listed here only in order to warn our readers that her 1971 published version of *The Book of Shadows* is garbled, illiterate and better ignored.

STONE, MERLIN—*The Paradise Papers, The Suppression of Women's Rites* (Virago Ltd., in association with Quartet Books, London, 1976)

SYKES, EGERTON (compiler)—*Everyman's Dictionary of Non-Classical Mythology* (J. M. Dent & Sons, London, 1968)

TRYON, THOMAS—*Harvest Home* (Hodder & Stoughton, London, 1974, and Coronet paperback, London, 1975)

VALIENTE, DOREEN—*Where Witchcraft Lives* (Aquarian Press, London, 1962)

VALIENTE, DOREEN—*An ABC of Witchcraft Past and Present* (Robert Hale, London, 1973)

VALIENTE, DOREEN—*Natural Magic* (Robert Hale, 1975)

VALIENTE, DOREEN—*Witchcraft for Tomorrow* (Robert Hale, 1978)

VOGH, JAMES—*The Thirteenth Zodiac; The Sign of Arachne* (Granada, St. Albans, 1979; first published as *Arachne Rising*, Hart-Davis, MacGibbon, London, 1977).

WARNER, MARINA—*Alone of All Her Sex—the Myth and the Cult of the Virgin Mary* (Weidenfeld & Nicolson, London, 1976)

WILDE, LADY—*Ancient Legends, Mystic Charms and Superstitions of Ireland* (Ward & Downey, London, 1888, reprinted in paperback by O'Gorman Ltd., Galway, 1971)

WILSON, ANNIE—*The Wise Virgin, the Missing Link Between Men and Women* (Turnstone Books, London, 1979)

WYATT, ISABEL—*Goddess into Saint; the Foster-Mother of Christ* (article in *The Golden Blade*, 1963, reprinted as booklet by Mitchell & Co., Arundel, Sussex)

Index

Some of these items (such as 'Circle', 'High Priestess', 'Candle') appear on almost every page; for these, we have listed only certain key references.

We have taken some arbitrary decisions whether to list some items under (e.g.) 'Celtic Cross' or 'Cross, Celtic'; if in doubt, look under both.

Individuals are listed generally under surnames (e.g. 'Jung, Carl G.'); but legendary, and some ancient, ones under the first element of their names as usually written (e.g. 'Fionn mac Cumhal', 'Maid Marian').